EXECUTIVE COACHING WORLD:

A GLOBAL PERSPECTIVE

www.executivecoachingworld.com

Executive Coaching World:
A Global Perspective

Results and analysis of the
world's largest global executive coaching survey.

A global view from 1,190 executive coaches
with over 8,000 years of experience that is a valuable asset for
practitioners, academics, teachers and trainers.

William Pennington

CHI TEACHING

For Alison

Thank you to the amazing people who have inspired me on my journey as a coach, I have learnt so much from you all:

Richard Bandler, Susanna Bellini, Michael Breen, Jackie Calderwood, Shelle Rose Charvet, Charles Faukner, Stephen Gilligan, John Grinder, Alison Hodge, *The* Ed Percival, John la Valle and Sally Vanson.

A big thank-you to Aboodi Shabi and Philippe Truffert who were fantastic to work with during the trial phase and to the more than 1,800 coaches, including almost 1,200 executive coaches, who took part in this research.

I hope that this book will help create better executive coaches who in turn will facilitate better leaders who in turn will help build a better future world for us all and especially for my daughters: Rachel, Katherine and Alice.

From my first book **Release the star within you** (ISBN: 0-9553658-0-5) and still one of my favourite quotes, as Thomas Edison said:

"If we did all the things we are capable of doing, we would literally astound ourselves."

Chapters

Appendices

Charts, Tables and Figures

Leadership Context

"As well as delivering value for our shareholders, our goal as a Group is to run our business in a responsible way. This means understanding the issues that matter most to our stakeholders and addressing them. This work provides the foundations of our Corporate Responsibility strategy. It enables all parts of the Group to effectively focus their efforts and resources on the most important issues. We rely on our people to deliver responsible business management through their daily actions and decisions." (Goodwin, 2007)

"Just 18 months on, the very same bank has set another record; this time by posting a loss of £28 billion, the biggest in British corporate history.....The demise of RBS can be summed up in just one word: greed. Under the stewardship of Sir Fred Goodwin, its former chief executive, RBS bought every bank and financial institution it could get its hands on, regardless of whether it made economic sense. Sir Fred, 50, became obsessed with his quest to make RBS a titan of world banking, and had such an overbearing personality that none of his staff had the clout to stop him, even when some of them began to have concerns that the bank was overstretching itself." (Rayner, 2009)

The role of organisations has become ever more important in the world with their leaders under more pressure and scrutiny than ever before. Over the last 20 years and against this backdrop a new profession has emerged called executive coaching, claiming to transform the performance of leaders and offer a significant return-on-investment. As a result of the benefits felt by executives and their organisations, executive coaching has seen rapid growth to what some claim is now a $2bn industry. (Passmore & Gibbes, 2007)

Yet executive coaching does not even have a universally accepted definition of what it is, let alone universally accepted standards and as a result, anyone may claim to be an executive coach and deliver any kind of service.   Organisations are beginning to ask for qualifications and accreditation but are still unsure what it is they are buying. The academic world has been slow to catch up with the explosion of practitioners; globally, some estimate there may be as many as 29,000 executive coaches. There have been only a handful of empirical studies with few having reliable methodology and academics have commented that the quality of research was extremely poor.   However they agree that defining and delineating the field is the most urgent task facing the industry as it moves towards professional status. (ICF, 2007)

There has perhaps never been a more pressing time for executives to need great executive coaches. As the complexity of the modern world unfolds, even the ways organisations are measured is changing; the *triple bottom line* is no longer considered simply a regulatory requirement but a positive competitive advantage. (Elkington, 2009)

It is leaders of organisations that have a responsibility not only to have the right words, but the right actions to back them up. Executive coaching has a significant role to play in developing todays and tomorrows leaders who can deliver a better future, not only as profit for all stakeholders, but a better future for the people and the planet impacted by the organisation.

Footnote

Recently, I was asked to make a presentation on the pedagogy (science of teaching) of leadership and coaching and was struck with the parallels between these connected worlds.

The traditional views of leadership seem to be shifting from one concerned with positional power and conspicuous accomplishment to one based on mutual understanding. There seen to be many definitions and descriptions available, but the one that works best for me (so far) is:

> "True leadership is creating a domain in which we continually learn and become more capable of participating in our unfolding future… where the capacity to discover and participate has more to do with our being – our total orientation of our character and consciousness …we and those around us continually deepen our understanding of reality and are able to participate in shaping the future." (Jaworski, 1996)

It is against this changing backdrop or perhaps because of it that executive coaching has come into being and why it now has such a vital role to play in the development of our future leaders.

William Pennington

Chapter 1

Introduction

The etymology of the word *coach* in the sense of meaning a large carriage dates back to the 16th century with its roots in Hungary, where it was derived from a town called Kocs. The first record of its usage akin to the current professional meaning was in the 19th century when it was used as university slang to describe a private tutor, or an instructor in sport and athletics. (The Concise Oxford Dictionary of English Etymology, 1996)

Executive is defined as "a person with senior managerial responsibility in a business"; where a *business* is understood to also include non-profit making organisations. (The Oxford Dictionary of English (revised edition), 2005)

The first critical literature review of *executive coaching* concluded that the term was formed in the early 1990s, but that the practice had an older history with consultants blending organisational development and psychology since the 1950s. It commented that since the mid-nineties there had been an increase in publications, establishment of professional associations (such as the International Coaching Federation (ICF)), and the industry had grown significantly. (Kampa-Kokesch & Anderson, 2001)

A study of coaching research between 1937 and 2003 reveals only 56 empirical studies, the majority of which were uncontrolled group or case studies with few having reliable methodology and concludes that the "quality of research was extremely poor". (Sherman & Freas, 2004)

Researchers (Feldman & Lankau, 2005; Grant & Cavanagh, 2004; Passmore & Gibbes, 2007) have suggested an agenda for future research which includes:

- Defining and delineating the field of executive coaching.

- What is the impact of executive coaching on performance?

- What are the methodologies and behaviours used in executive coaching and which work?

This research seeks to both define and delineate executive coaching and investigate the behaviours used.

Aim

The aim of this research is to create a definition of executive coaching in English that can be universally accepted by executive coaches and to investigate how English speaking executive coaches behave linguistically.

This research is with English speaking executive coaches because the topics under consideration have a significant linguistic dimension and it was not feasible to create definitions and conduct the survey in multiple languages. Any data from coaches who do not primarily coach in English would have seriously questioned the validity of the results and were excluded from the sample.

Context

There are plenty of definitions of executive coaching from practitioners, coaching suppliers, academics and coaching bodies that serve to complicate and confuse. Executive coaching is approaching its 18th birthday, so it seems a good time to define its adult identity! A clear and agreed definition would be a significant step forward towards a professional industry.

The coaching conversation is at the heart of good executive coaching and therefore the effective use of language is one of the most critical skills that a great executive coach can possess. It is perhaps surprising that prior to this research, there has been no research that focuses specifically on this aspect of the coaching process.

There are thoughts and models about linguistic behaviours of executive coaches put forward by coaching teachers and anecdotal evidence from practitioners and academics. There are some qualitative surveys of overall coaching competencies and skills that do include some references to linguistic behaviours, but it is the aim of this systematic quantitative and qualitative research to create a solid foundation for future investigation into this critical dimension of executive coaching.

Chapter 2

Methodology

On one hand the research questions and literature review suggest that a verifiable definition of executive coaching and a clear unequivocal understanding of linguistic behaviours are required.

However on the other hand, executive coaching is a complex domain involving two multifaceted human beings exhibiting complex behaviours set within an intricate system and that any linguistic definition will be based on the interpretation of the language used and could be highly subjective.

These paradoxical points of view, lead to a conclusion that the best approach to this research should be taken from a pragmatic paradigm and utilise a mixed methodology. According to Tashakkori & Teddlie, (1998):

> "Study what interests you and is of value to you, study in the different ways in which you deem appropriate, and use the results in ways that can bring about positive consequences within your value system ."

There is a growing movement that considers that a pragmatic and mixed approach will lead to better research in the social sciences. Researchers should choose the best method and approach based on their questions instead of the polarity of quantitative and qualitative research. (Johnson & Onwuegbuzie, 2004; Sechrest & Sidani, 1995; Viadero, 2005)

Johnson & Onwuegbuzie, (2004) conclude that:

> "By narrowing the divide between quantitative and qualitative researchers, mixed methods research has a great potential to promote a shared responsibility in the quest for attaining accountability for educational quality. The time has come for mixed methods research."

In order to test a universally accepted definition it was necessary to have a global reach and considering available resources, a concurrent mixed method strategy and an on-line survey instrument were used to collect primarily quantitative data and draw conclusions about the population from the sample using statistical analysis. The results were then analysed in order to answer the questions, test the hypotheses and to investigate relationships between independent and dependent variables. (Creswell, 2003)

An alternative would have been a pure quantitative approach that would test a universally accepted definition but miss an opportunity to collect richer data that would clarify some existing confusions, develop new concepts and hypotheses. Another would have been to use a fully qualitative approach with more detailed and in-depth evaluation of the concepts; however the resulting small sample size would have led to poor statistical validity and therefore no universal acceptability of the hypotheses.

On-line survey technology was chosen because it is well developed; the vast majority of the population have published email addresses and it was feasible to conduct a global survey with the available resources. A couple of services were tested and Survey Methods chosen as it has a more flexible and powerful design capability. The on-line survey in Appendix A was designed to qualify practicing executive coaches; collect independent variables of where they lived (location), their business background (background) and how long they have been practicing executive coaching (experience); and collect opinion about and information regarding their practice (Saunders, Lewis, & Thornhill, 2006; surveymethods.com, 2008)

The qualitative data collected in the survey was designed to give more clarity to the quantitative data, add richness and to assist in the analysis, testing and development of the hypotheses.   The figure below (2-1) shows the coding and analysis process used in this research. (Creswell, 2009)

Figure 2-1 Qualitative data analysis method

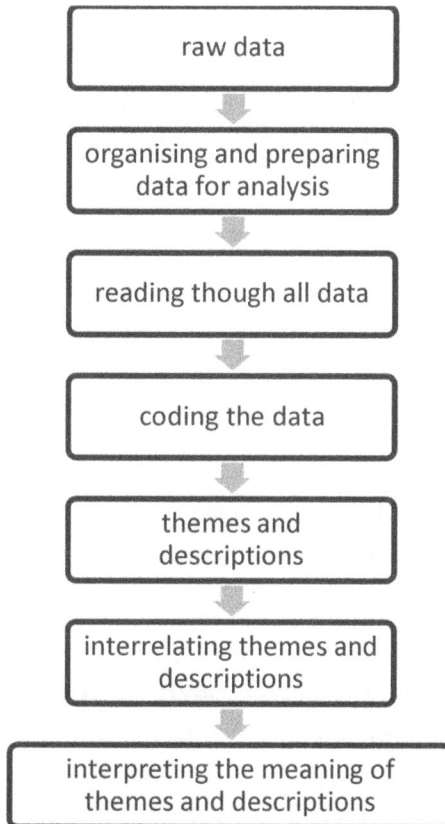

```
┌─────────────────────────────┐
│          raw data           │
└─────────────────────────────┘
               ↓
┌─────────────────────────────┐
│   organising and preparing  │
│      data for analysis      │
└─────────────────────────────┘
               ↓
┌─────────────────────────────┐
│    reading though all data  │
└─────────────────────────────┘
               ↓
┌─────────────────────────────┐
│       coding the data       │
└─────────────────────────────┘
               ↓
┌─────────────────────────────┐
│        themes and           │
│       descriptions          │
└─────────────────────────────┘
               ↓
┌─────────────────────────────┐
│  interrelating themes and   │
│       descriptions          │
└─────────────────────────────┘
               ↓
┌─────────────────────────────┐
│ interpreting the meaning of │
│   themes and descriptions   │
└─────────────────────────────┘
```

Content validity was checked by running a small trial in which executive coaches were asked to complete the survey and then undertake face-to-face interviews to test their views and opinions in more depth. Construct validity is important in this research as many of the variables concern executive coaches' opinions about concepts such as *relevance* and *agreement* and other concepts from the literature review may have ambiguous meanings. These were checked for validity using the small trial, analysing the qualitative data and conducting consistency checks. (Hair, 2003)

Reliability was assessed using alternative forms; and four pairs and one triplet of questions were used to measure equivalent forms of a construct. (Appendix B).

Reliability and validity was checked by collecting qualitative data that is used to check quantitative answers, code into existing categories or create new ones, and to provide clarity on the understanding of concepts. The right to left order of ranking was reversed so that inaccurate responses could be identified and removed. The survey software was configured to present relevant questions in random order to remove any order bias and to conduct relevant data integrity checks. (Saunders et al., 2006)

The data collected from the survey was transferred from 'Survey Methods' to 'Microsoft Excel' for initial data cleaning, initial analysis and charting, then to 'SPSS' for more advanced statistical analysis and charting.

Sampling

The population of interest are executive coaches practicing in the English language. However the literature review illustrated that there are no agreed definitions of what executive coaching is and that in this unregulated industry, currently anyone may purport to be an executive coach. There are many coaches around the world and a large proportion of them claim to have an interest in executive coaching but how many are practicing executive coaches? (Feldman & Lankau, 2005; ICF, 2007)

The sampling technique chosen was to create a frame of all English speaking coaches that will include a random sample of the population and then qualify practicing English speaking executive coaches to make up the sample. (Mador, 2006)

A frame of 12,500 coaches was created from members of ICF; Association of Coaching; WABC; British Psychological Society SIG in Coaching and Graduate Directory of Certified Master Coaches; those that work for leading suppliers including the *50 Top Executive Coaches*; and those registered with other sources on the internet. This frame was built with coaches identified as being from the major English speaking countries.

Invitations were sent by email to associates and members of DBM and EMCC. Links to the survey were published via Euro Coach List, International Coaching Register, IAC and APECS.

The table below (2-3) shows the population estimates from the most extensive global coaching survey conducted so far by the ICF and a more recent survey that claimed an error of 2.7% on a sample of 786 predominantly US and Canadian executive coaches.

Table 2-3 Population Estimates from Historical Surveys

Population estimates	ICF 2006 low estimate	ICF 2006 high estimate	Sherpa 2008
Global coach	30,000	50,000	n/a
Global executive coach (58%)	17,400	29,000	n/a
English speaking (78%) executive coach	14,000	23,000	n/a
US (50%) executive coach	8,700	14,500	5,000

In conclusion the lower ICF estimate was used and the global population of English speaking executive coaches in 2008 was estimated to be 14,000. (Corbett, 2008; ICF, 2007b)

The expected response rate from an internet based survey was 10% and that approximately half would be randomly selected executive coaches. Therefore the anticipated sample of 625 cases would equate to a margin of error between 3 and 5 per cent for a population of 14,000 at 95% level of certainty. (Saunders et al., 2006)

A sampling approach was designed to ensure that there was a random chance of an executive coach being included in the sample. However a number of factors may have impacted the randomness of the sample: the frame represents 30-42% of all English speaking coaches globally and may have been skewed to include or exclude more executive coaches; all coaches in the frame were invited to take part in the survey in order to achieve less than 5% error; and given the anticipated low response rate of on-line surveys there will be a large degree of self selection in the process.

In conclusion, based on analysis of other research (see Chapter 3) and non selected cases, the evidence suggests that this is a probability sample so inferences about the population may be made.

Response to the on-line survey of 1,834 was higher than predicted (15%), and also included a higher proportion of practicing English speaking executive coaches (65%). The sample was selected based on answers to questions 4, 7, 20 and 21. Those cases that did not coach in English (33), complete the survey (306), were not actively engaged in executive coaching in their practice (360), were students (6), or if they had been coaching for less than 2 years and spend less than 10% of their time practicing executive coaching (14) were excluded.

The resulting sample of 1,190 practicing English speaking executive coaches selected for the analysis equates to a margin of error of less than 3% for the estimated population of 14,000 at 95% level of certainty. (Saunders et al., 2006)

Data Coding, Cleaning and Analysis

The data was coded automatically by the on-line system which directly converted nominal and ordinal data into numbers. The data was then transferred to 'Microsoft Excel', where the conversion was checked and cleaned to ensure a robust set of data. A full breakdown of the coding and cleaning process can be found in Appendix B.

Chapter 3 includes a demographic data analysis that compares the results with other surveys to highlight differences and similarities, with the aim of increasing validity and testing for any sampling errors.

The quantitative data was analysed initially using charts to identify interesting differences or trends between the categories of independent variables within the sets of dependent variables. The data was then tested for normal distribution to see whether parametric tests could be deployed. The frequency distribution is charted using histograms, followed by a 'Kolmogorov-Smirnov' test for normality of data and a 'Levene' test for homogeneous of variances. If the data is **not** from a normalised population then a non-parametric 'Kruskal-Wallis' test was used with 'Mann-Whitney' follow up tests with a 'Bonferroni' correction applied. When a normalised population was concluded, analysis was undertaken using 'ANOVA' to identify groups where there were some statistically significant differences in means, with a follow up 'Tukey' test to identify the specific group pairs. (Field, 2005; Hair, 2003)

Demographics

Location of Executive Coaches

The chart below (3-1) shows where executive coaches live. However as the number of executive coaches in New Zealand, Ireland, South Africa, Europe and Other were each less than 30, it was determined that any demographic analysis would be statistically invalid, therefore they were

Chart 3-1 Where executive coaches live

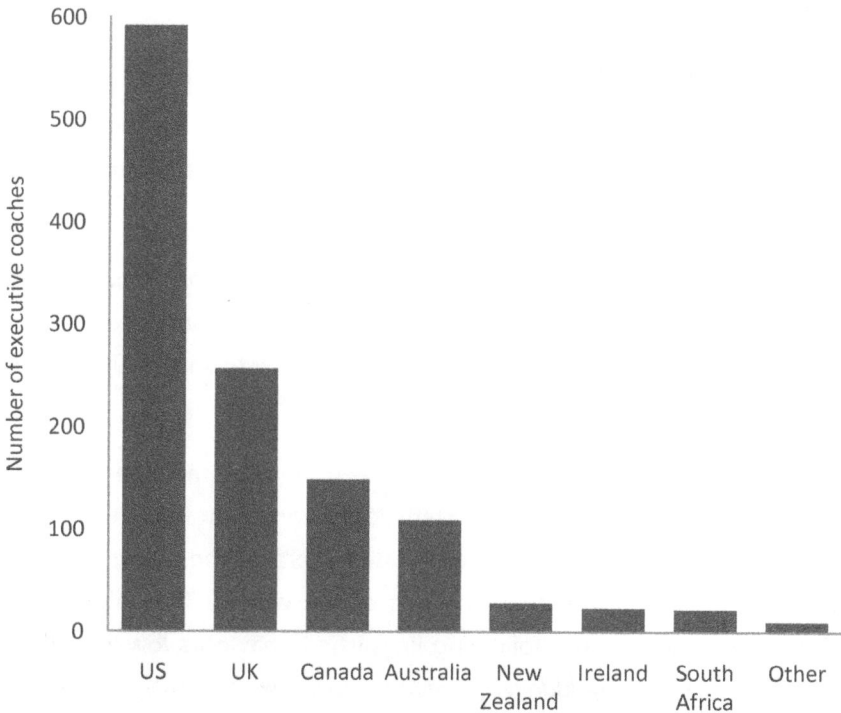

Chart 3-2 Location of executive coaches

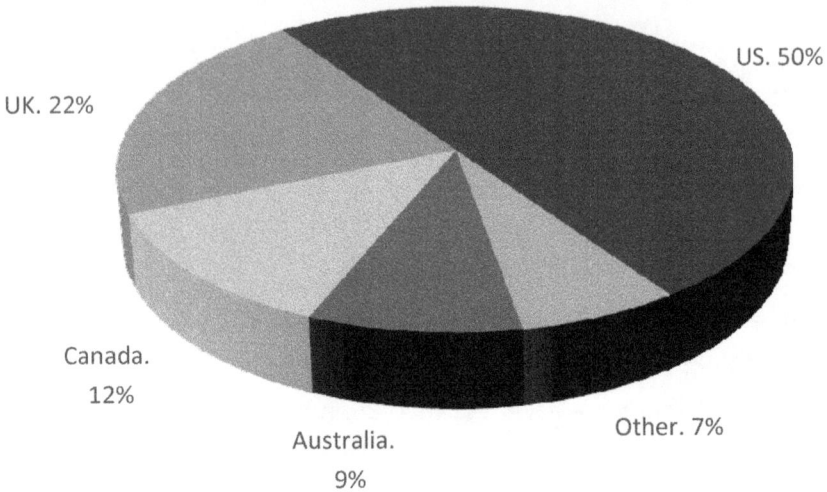

US. 50%

UK. 22%

Canada.
12%

Australia.
9%

Other. 7%

combined together for the group analysis as shown in the chart above (3-2). (Saunders et al., 2006)

Demographic comparison with other surveys

The chart opposite (3-3) compares the results for the location where executive coaches live with two surveys conducted by Sherpa and the ICF. (Corbett, 2009; ICF, 2007)

The Sherpa survey is predominantly US centric research. This research (Pennington 2009) shows a significantly higher UK response than the ICF survey, that may have been caused by high growth in the UK market (Gray, 2006), or home country bias of the researcher.

However analysis of the differences between the UK sample and the rest of the world shows that the only statistically significant impact was that executive coaches who live in the UK rated *a form of consulting* and *one-to-one counselling* lower than the rest of the world. They also speak slightly less and rate the following linguistic behaviours lower: *telling, instructing, offering guidance, providing ideas, being a role model* and *paraphrasing.* In conclusion the larger UK sample may have had some impact on the results for relevance of linguistic behaviours – decreasing the ratings for more directive behaviours; although this impact may be small as the UK rates almost all variables lower than the rest of the world.

Chart 3-3 Comparison of surveys and location where samples live

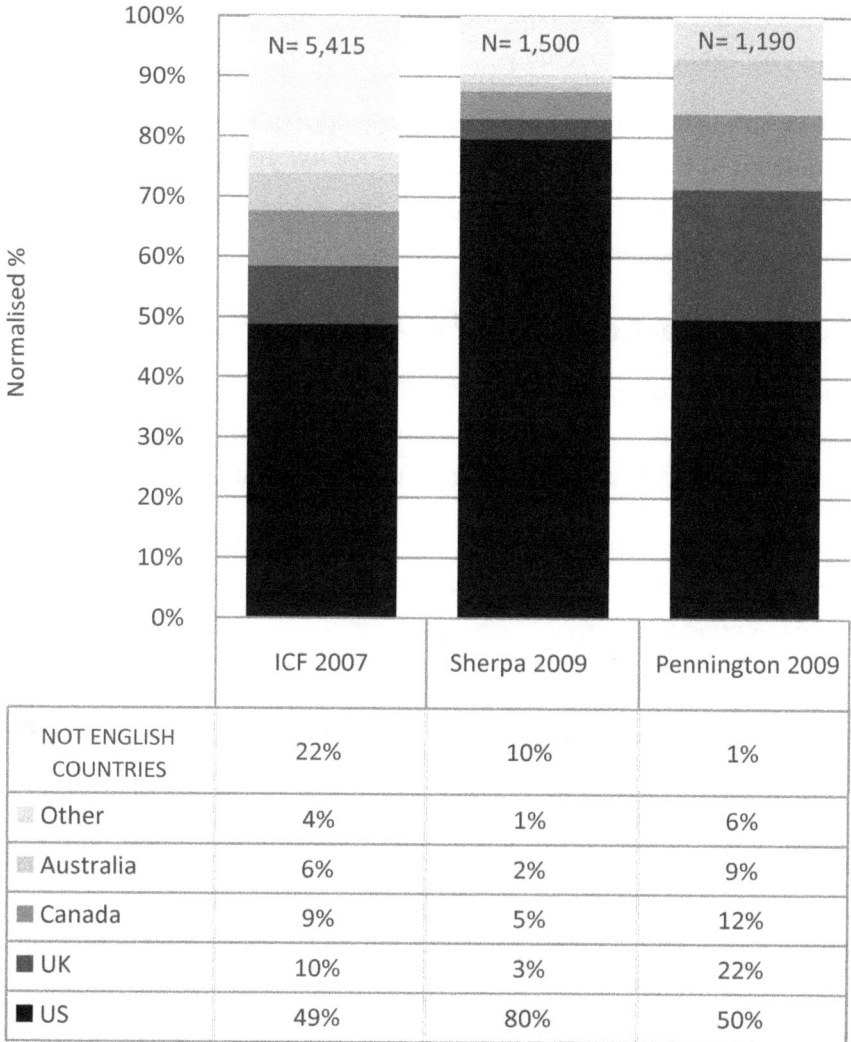

	ICF 2007	Sherpa 2009	Pennington 2009
NOT ENGLISH COUNTRIES	22%	10%	1%
Other	4%	1%	6%
Australia	6%	2%	9%
Canada	9%	5%	12%
UK	10%	3%	22%
US	49%	80%	50%

The ICF survey included 58% who listed their coaching speciality as executive coaching however no definition or selection criteria were published. The Sherpa survey included 55% executive coaches and although a definition was published, no selection criteria were indicated. In an earlier survey from Sherpa (Corbett, 2008) the criteria broadly included *executive and business coaches* that if also used for the Sherpa 2009 survey would question the validity of any results claiming to be purely for executive coaching.

The sample in this survey was selected to include 100% executive coaches as defined in the selection criteria (see Chapter 2) and would represent 78% of the global multi-lingual population, using the ICF demographic profile to extrapolate the results.

Business Background of Executive Coaches

The chart opposite (3-4) shows that a significant majority (>70%) of executive coaches are from a business background: either as an executive, consultant or both; or from HR, L&D or training.

Some former managers do not consider they were senior enough to be called executive, neither rather surprisingly, did some HR Directors but were re-coded that way.

It was noted that the number of executive coaches with either a clinical or occupational psychology background is low (9%).   Liljenstrand conducted a survey of 928 US based coaches showing that 18% had occupational psychology, 23% clinical psychology and 50% business academic backgrounds. The differences may be caused by coaches following a different career after college, geographic differences, changes in the market since 2003, or that the survey was only a third executive coaches. Further analysis reveals that a total of 2,361 coaches undertook the survey but most did not meet the criteria for these academic

Chart 3-4 Business background of executive coaches

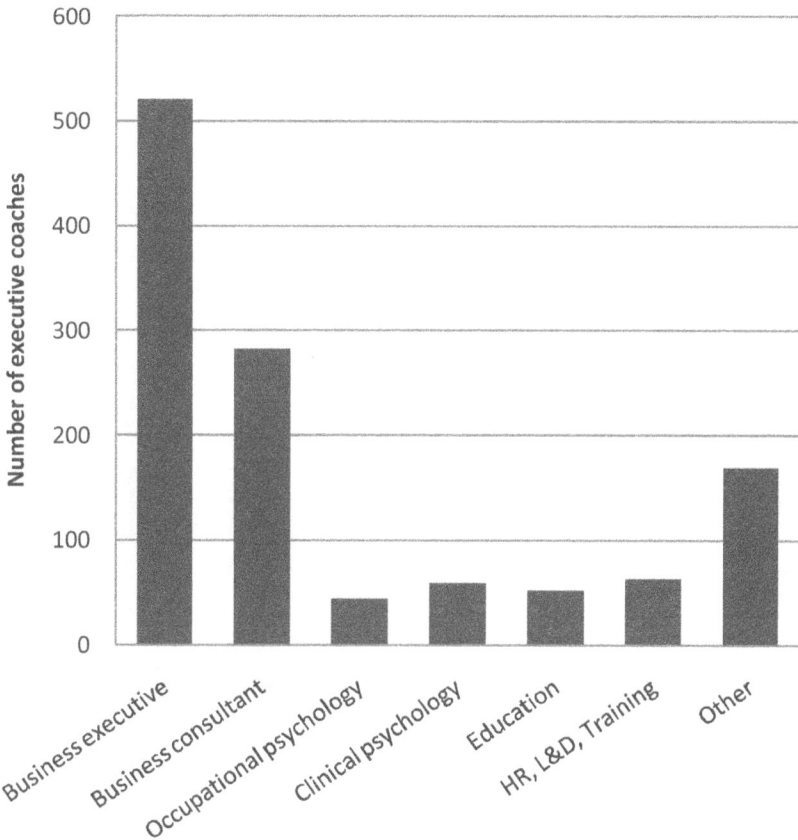

backgrounds. The adjusted results for academic backgrounds are 7% occupational psychology and 9% clinical psychology. (Liljenstrand, 2004)

In conclusion, the low number of practicing executive coaches with a clinical and occupational psychology background in the sample may be representative of the population.

Experience of Executive Coaches

It is noted from the chart below (3-5) that the sample confirms executive coaching is a growing profession. Using the midpoints of the ranges (and 12.5 for 10+ years) the total experience represented in this survey is over 8,000 years.

Chart 3-5 Experience of executive coaches

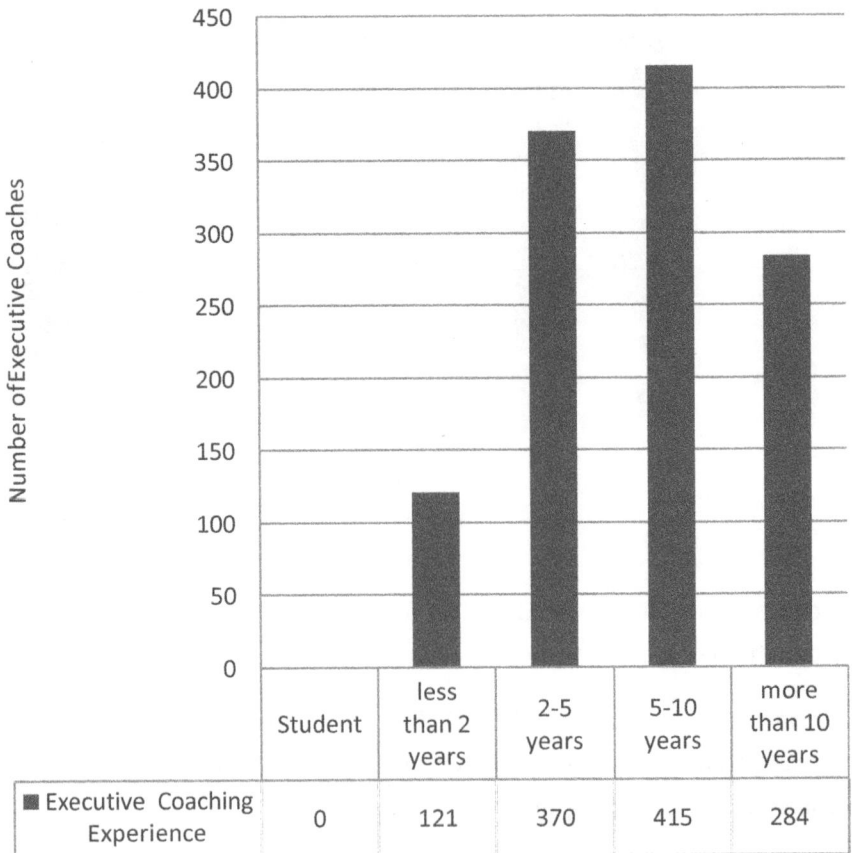

	Student	less than 2 years	2-5 years	5-10 years	more than 10 years
■ Executive Coaching Experience	0	121	370	415	284

Executive Coaches' Practicing Time

The chart and table below (3-6 and 3-7) confirm that executive coaching is the most practiced activity for this sample, which is good given that this is meant to be a representative sample of the population of executive coaches!

Chart 3-6 Executive coaches' practicing time

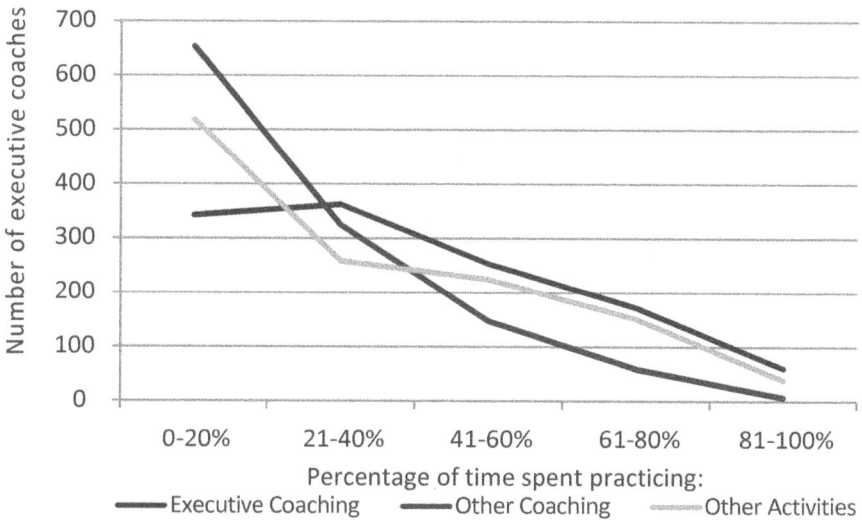

Table 3-7 Executive coaches' practicing time

	Executive Coaching	Other Coaching	Other Activities
N	1190	1190	1190
Mean	40.85%	25.15%	34.00%
99% Confidence Interval for Mean:			
Lower Bound	39.03%	23.61%	32.07%
Upper Bound	42.67%	26.69%	35.93%
Std. Deviation	24.334	20.608	25.802

Chapter 4

A Definition

An extensive review of the literature has shown that there is no generally accepted definition of executive coaching. This may be due to the eclectic nature of this emerging profession where the majority of executive coaches come from a wide range of business, occupational psychology and clinical psychology backgrounds. (Liljenstrand, 2004)

The task of defining and delineating the field is the first and most basic challenge facing the whole coaching industry as it moves towards a professional status. (Grant & Cavanagh, 2004)

The dictionary definition given earlier of an *executive* stated that it is someone with senior managerial responsibility, but what constitutes *senior* and is this matched by those who receive *executive coaching*?

Reeves states that executive coaching is for a Chairman, CEO and other senior leaders. He then slightly confusingly describes these together as the *executive team* and/or *corporate management team*. An ICF conference on executive coaching described senior as being "a key contributor who has a powerful position in the organisation". Kilburg defines an executive as someone who has managerial authority and responsibility. (Kampa-Kokesch & Anderson, 2001; Kilburg, 1996; Reeves, 2006)

Unusually Thompson et al. chose not to use the term *executive coaching* to describe coaching for middle managers. However an annual survey run by Sherpa showed that at least in the Unites States, 42% of organisations make executive coaching available to managers at all levels. (Corbett, 2009; Thompson, Purdy, & Summers, 2008)

In seems therefore that Kilburn's definition that executive coaching is for all managers with authority and responsibility in an organisation does apply.

There have been numerous attempts to create a definitive definition for executive coaching that also add to the confusion. (Tang & Meuse, 2007)

Executive coaching is described as :

- a helping relationship (Kilburg, 1996)
- a method that can be applied as part of a consulting intervention, i.e. it's a form of consulting (Stern, 2004)
- a branch of organisational psychology (Orenstein, 2006)
- a key element of the relationship is one-to-one counselling about work issues. (Feldman & Lankau, 2005)
- usually underpinned by human psychological (especially psychotherapeutic) theories (but suggests an alternative based on adult learning theory, where coaching is seen as a "transformative learning process"). (Gray,2006)
- on a continuum between counselling and consulting. (Joo, 2005)

Joo also suggests the following definition based on his thorough analysis of the literature:

"Executive coaching is a process of a one-to-one relationship between a professional coach and executive (coachee) for the purpose of enhancing coachee's behavioural change through self-awareness and learning, and thus ultimately for the success of the individual and organisation."

However this does not explain the role of the organisation, the process, the nature of the relationship, and perhaps most importantly what an executive coach actually does. It is also not clear what *enhancing coachee's behavioural change* actually means.

The role of the organisation in the executive coaching process is one of stakeholder or sponsor. This creates a triangular relationship that sometimes can be complex and a source of friction. There may even be ethical or contractual implications between these three parties. (Natale & Diamante, 2005; Orenstein, 2002; Sherman & Freas, 2004)

It seems that this triangular or 'triadic relationship' is a defining characteristic of executive coaching.

Academics define executive coaching as a theoretically grounded, systematic and goal-orientated process that is designed to facilitate sustained change in skills development, performance enhancement and personal development. They describe the relationship between a coach and executive as a collaborative equal partnership. (Grant & Cavanagh, 2004; Natale & Diamante, 2005)

Others describe executive coaches as change agents that create a safe environment to allow people to develop themselves. They facilitate analysis and solutions in a process of assisted self-exploration. This in turn leads to self-awareness and self-improvement for the executive. (Gray, 2006; Hieker & Huffington, 2006; Reeves, 2006)

Practitioners explain that Executive coaching is essentially a dialogue-based facilitative learning process that is all about asking questions and at its best, almost invisible. (Feldman & Lankau, 2005; Tang & Meuse, 2007; Thomson, 2003)

Research Questions and Hypotheses

Question 1

What is a definition of executive coaching that can be accepted by most English speaking executive coaches?

Hypothesis 1 is that 80% of practicing executive coaches will agree with the proposed definition:

> *"Executive coaching is a facilitated learning process within a triadic relationship between a professional coach, an executive and their organisation. An executive coach acts as the facilitative change-agent primarily working one-to-one with the executive in a collaborative equal partnership, with a purpose to create sustained change in the executive's skills, behaviour and performance so that both the executive and their organisation get ultimate benefit."*

Question 2

Who receives executive coaching?

Hypothesis 2 is that all managers in an organisation can receive executive coaching.

Results and Analysis

There were a couple of executive coaches who questioned the value of creating a definition. One fundamentally disagrees with the presumption that there is (or should be) a definition! While the other suggests that each client should create their own definition. It is interesting to speculate how their executive coaching clients know what it is they are buying!

The remaining 1,188 coaches willingly contributed to the quantitative analysis, including 325 coaches who provided over 14,000 words of qualitative input.

From the qualitative data there appears to be a small number of coaches who relate executive coaching to other forms of coaching in various different ways. They say that executive coaching is:

- not the same as performance coaching

- similar to business coaching but for executives

- above business coaching (which is triadic)

- in the middle between business and life coaching

- and includes organisational coaching, which is broader in approach and audience

One suggesting that this survey is about corporate coaching not executive coaching.

Gale et al. report there is no clear distinction between the many different labels used to describe many sectors of coaching. Although personal, executive, life and business are identified as most commonly used. They conclude that many of these labels describe the same niche. (Gale, Liljenstrand, Pardieu, & Nebeker, 2002)

Several executive coaches mention team coaching, also referring to it as group or organisational coaching. While some believe executive coaching includes team coaching of senior managers, others propose that it is more aligned with training and other organisational development programs. As they share many of the same paradigms, an executive coach may well deliver team coaching to the group and then executive coaching to the individuals.

Who receives Executive Coaching?

The chart opposite (4-1) shows that there is almost total agreement that *board members, directors and CXOs* and *senior managers* receive executive coaching.

There was strong support that *managers at all levels* and *specialists without management responsibility* can also receive executive coaching. However there was significantly low or no agreement to suggest that *anyone in an organisation, anyone* or *business owners* receive executive coaching.

The qualitative analysis reveals that when coaches answered *anyone*, they may be taking a very broad understanding of the term *executive* as anyone who has to execute, manage and lead and may include business owners and "home makers" in this group. Others took an alternative view that executive coaching was for *senior managers* and *executives* but regardless of their current career status or the purpose for coaching, e.g. between jobs, planning retirement or setting up their own business.

There were some executive coaches who took the view that junior managers looking to move up the organisation, those in succession plans and those seeking to improve their work relationships also may receive executive coaching.

In summary, this survey demonstrates that executive coaching is for senior managers and leaders in organisations, with more junior managers

Chart 4-1 Who receives executive coaching?

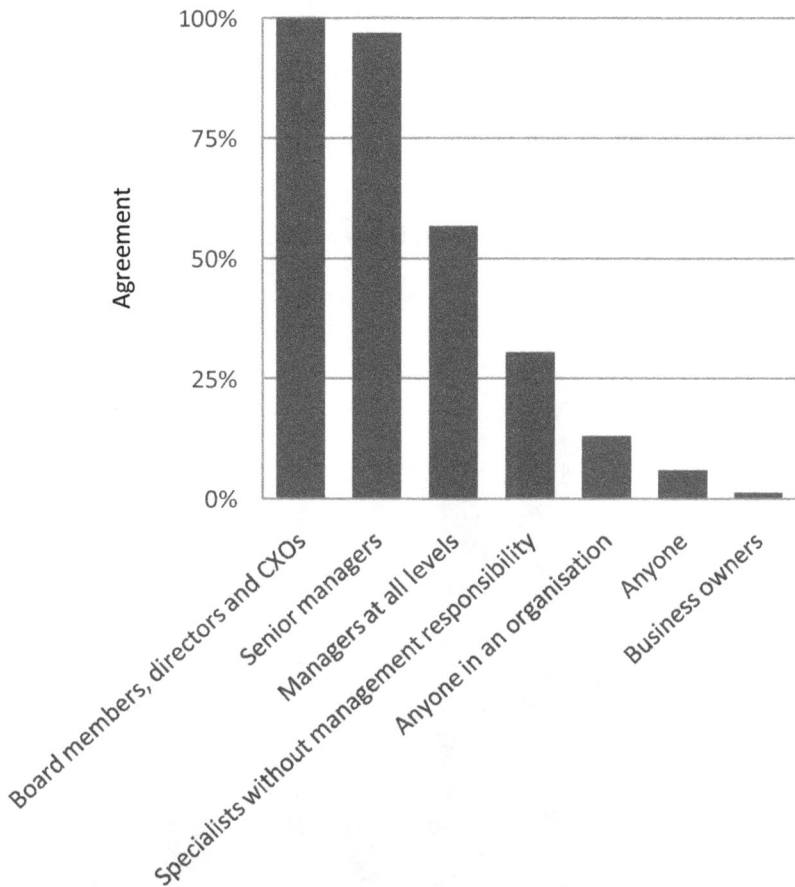

also often receiving it and occasionally specialists without management responsibility.   However as one executive coach asked with a very pertinent question "Does this mean it is no longer executive coaching if the organisation is not involved?" The answer to this will be explored later in this chapter when discussing the triadic relationship.

What is Executive Coaching?

In the chart below (4-3) each shade of black represents the number of executive coaches that scored each category (i.e. a specific definition) with a particular score; for example around 43% of executive coaches gave *a facilitated learning process* a score of 10. Overall the chart may be

Chart 4-3 What is executive coaching?

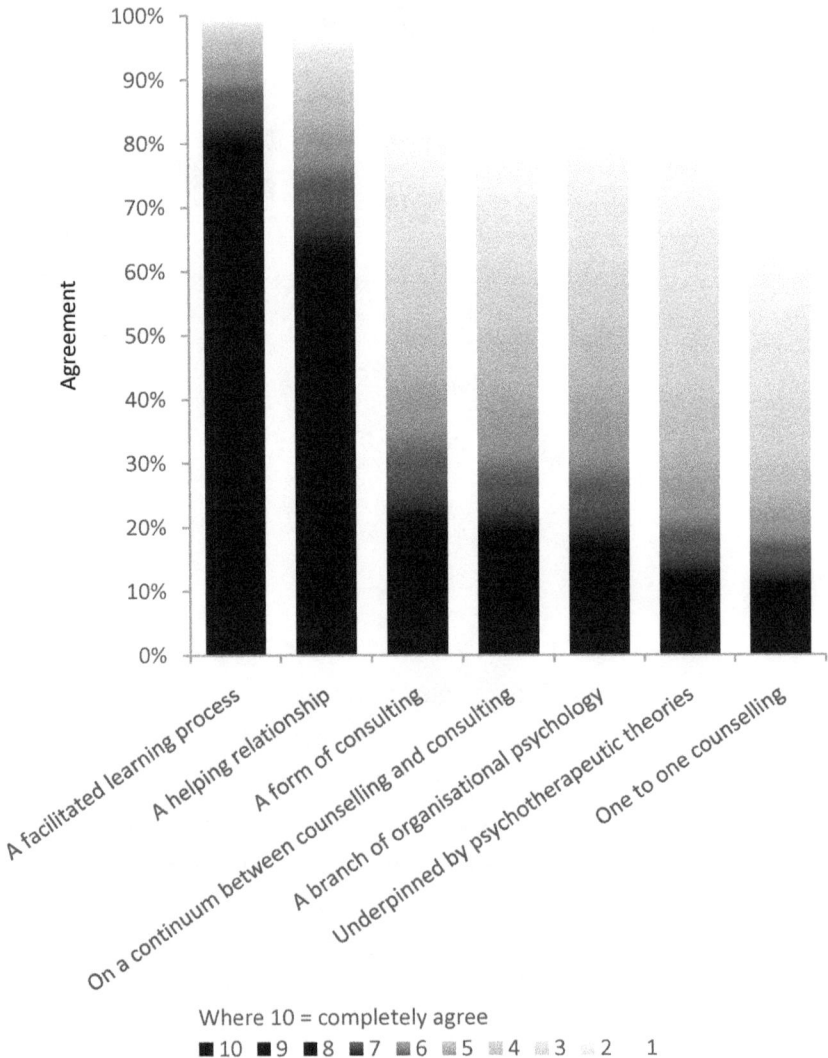

Where 10 = completely agree

■10 ■9 ■8 ■7 ■6 ▪5 ▪4 ▪3 ▪2 ▪1

interpreted by looking at the darkness; the greater the area of darker colour, the more agreement there is with a particular definition.

Initial interpretation of this chart shows significantly high agreement with the definitions of executive coaching as *a facilitated learning process* and *a helping relationship*; and significantly lower agreement (i.e. disagreement) with all the other definitions.

The gap between the two accepted definitions and the rest is confirmed by comparing the mean, median and mode in the table below (4-2). It is interesting to note that the more psychological or therapeutic the definitions become, the less support they obtain.

Table 4-2 What is executive coaching?

Executive coaching is	N	Mean	99% Confidence Interval for Mean:		Standard Deviation	Median	Mode
			Lower Bound	Upper Bound			
A facilitated learning process	1158	8.56	8.375	8.673	1.875	9	10
A helping relationship	1155	7.57	7.334	7.742	2.583	8	10
A form of consulting	1136	4.55	4.269	4.713	2.848	4	1
On a continuum between counselling and consulting	1131	4.34	4.083	4.499	2.794	4	1
A branch of organizational psychology	1126	4.33	4.042	4.478	2.661	4	1
Underpinned by psycho-therapeutic theories	1125	3.76	3.536	3.924	2.491	3	1
One-to-one counselling	1130	3.2	2.942	3.338	2.569	2	1

Where 10 = completely agree

The qualitative analysis shows that most executive coaches are adamant that there should be clear distinction between executive coaching and therapy, counselling and consulting, with clear, very distinct and important differentials between them. Executive coaching is its own discipline with a unique process, different focus and expected outcomes.

Executive coaches are also clear that if therapy or counselling is required, they would refer a client to a professional in those areas.

A few acknowledge that these fields are related and that there may be techniques and skills that can be leveraged between them, although there are mixed views on how useful therapy or psychological frameworks might be in an executive coaching context. One coach suggests that it is much more than psychology and that an executive coach requires solid knowledge of business, law, regulation and real world economics. (*Ed. - see Chapter 11 for a bonus paper about the competencies required by an excellent executive coach!*)

There are also a few coaches who propose that some consulting practices may be used in executive coaching, providing the practice is managed so that the executive coach is explicit when they take on a mentoring role and use their expertise to provide answers.

Some expanded on the concept of the *facilitated learning process* suggesting that executive coaching is facilitating an executive to define themselves: what they want, who they are and what they do; to realise their own potential and facilitating the answers and solutions.

Others proposed a definition themed around a quite different dimension of creating an environment in which this learning occurs. They suggest that executive coaching is creating the *space* for personal exploration; reflecting; deepening awareness of self, actions, behaviours, etc.; and change in which the executive coach can evoke and draw out the executive's wisdom.

The most popular definitions as shown earlier in Chart 4-3, use two different verbs *help* and *facilitate* and it is useful to explore their meanings.

In British English *help* means "offering someone services or material aid to make it easier or possible for them to do something" whereas *facilitate* is simply "making an action or process easy or easier". The meanings are similar although there is the distinction that helping suggest more involvement. This is clearer in American English definitions where *help* is "to give assistance or support to someone, to be of use to them or to further their advancement", whereas *facilitate* as well as meaning "making easier" also means "to help bring about". In conclusion, there is a more directive and participatory flavour to the word *helping* as well as connotations of therapy and counselling. (The Oxford Dictionary of English (revised edition), 2005; Merriam-Webster, 2009a)

In summary, the use of *a helping relationship* although gaining much support as a definition of executive coaching does not differentiate it from therapeutic and consulting practices and while a *facilitated learning process* gains the highest support amongst executive coaches, there were some suggestions that is could be more descriptive and include a new concept of space.

A Definition of Executive Coaching

In the chart below (4-5) each shade of black represents the number of executive coaches that rate each aspect of the definition with a particular level of agreement. Overall the chart may be interpreted by looking at the darkness; the greater the area of darker colour the more agreement there is with a particular part of the definition.

This chart shows that over 80% agree or strongly agree, with three parts of the definition. Only the first part "a triadic relationship" scored less, with only 70% either agreeing or strongly agreeing.

Chart 4-5 A definition of executive coaching

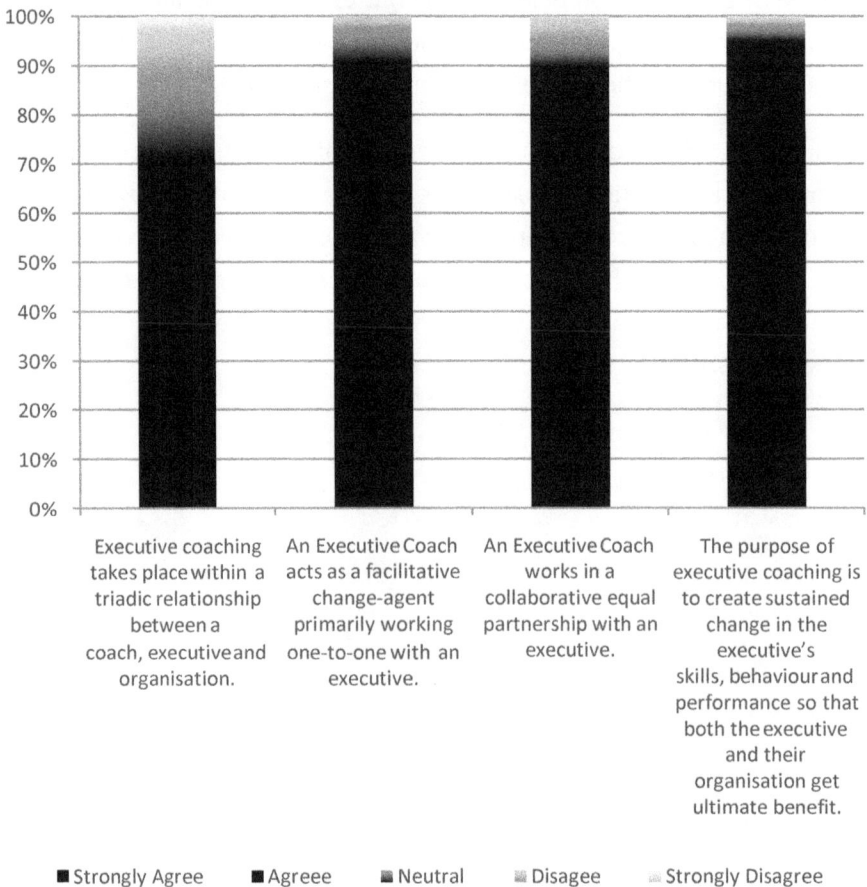

| | Executive coaching takes place within a triadic relationship between a coach, executive and organisation. | An Executive Coach acts as a facilitative change-agent primarily working one-to-one with an executive. | An Executive Coach works in a collaborative equal partnership with an executive. | The purpose of executive coaching is to create sustained change in the executive's skills, behaviour and performance so that both the executive and their organisation get ultimate benefit. |

■ Strongly Agree   ■ Agreee   ■ Neutral   ▦ Disagee   ▦ Strongly Disagree

The table (4-4) below confirms these findings and indicates there is good statistical evidence (99% confidence interval for mean) to conclude that this is a good representation of the population.

Table 4-4 A definition of executive coaching

	Executive Coaching takes place within a triadic relationship between a coach, executive and organisation.	An Executive Coach acts as a facilitative change-agent working primarily one-to-one with an executive.	An Executive Coach works in a collaborative equal partnership with an executive.	The purpose of Executive Coaching is to create sustained change in the executive's skills, behaviour and performance so that both the executive and their organisation get ultimate benefit.
N	1163	1163	1163	1163
Mean	2.16	1.54	1.56	1.30
99% Confidence Interval for Mean:				
Lower Bound	2.08	1.49	1.50	1.25
Upper Bound	2.24	1.59	1.62	1.35
Std. Deviation	1.051	0.723	0.827	0.623
Median	2	1	1	1
Mode	2	1	1	1

Where 1= strongly agree and 5=strongly disagree

The qualitative analysis is structured around each aspect of the definition, as follows:

"Executive coaching takes place within a triadic relationship between a coach, executive and organisation."

This topic is also one of the most prevalent in the qualitative data and analysis shows there are two recurring themes. Firstly, that executive coaching includes situations where the executive may contract with a coach directly and therefore the relationship would be strictly *dyadic*. Secondly, there is concern that the triadic relationship defines a role for the organisation that might compromise the coaching process.

Within this first theme there were some confusing descriptions. Most agree that the organisation usually contracts for the coaching, but occasionally it's the executive; even if the goal is still to improve the executive's performance in the organisation. Two pieces of research suggest that less than 10% may choose to pay for coaching directly and one proposes that it occurs to guarantee more privacy. (Alvey & Barclay, 2007; Corbett, 2009)

One executive coach says it is typically triadic, another says rarely, but most who make a comment say it depends. When it comes to explaining what it depends on, there are some quite surprising results.

Some executive coaches are very explicit about what constitutes *a direct contract* defining that the executive uses their own resources (time and money). Although in one case it is not clear whether an executive's own budget means personal or organisational funds.

However some executive coaches cite situations where the organisation should not be considered as a dimension in the relationship regardless of whether it is the organisation's time and money that is being used for the coaching programme. These include situations where the coach is approached without the involvement of the organisation or the executive "hires, commissions, partners, enlists, or chooses" the coach directly. However one coach was more direct about this:

> "an executive may choose to work one-on-one with the coach and not involve any other representatives of the organisation, even if the organisation pays for it."

Other coaches think that "needs analysis, coaching content and desired objectives" are criteria to decide whether it is a triadic relationship or not. They view that the organisation does not have a significant role to play in the relationship and some suggest that also includes the benefits that are gained from the coaching. One coach says:

"the sole purpose is to support, empower and develop the individual being coached, regardless of whether it benefits the organisation."

These views, although from a small minority, raise a serious ethical question. There does seem to be a need for more clarity around triadic coaching situations, however the ICF is already fairly clear about this in its code of ethics:

"In all cases, coaching engagement contracts or agreements should clearly establish the rights, roles, and responsibilities for both the client and sponsor if they are not the same persons.

The "sponsor" is the entity (including its representatives) paying for and/or arranging for coaching services to be provided." *(ICF, 2008)*

In summary there does seem to be a need for even more clarity around the content or interpretation of the ethics that define the organisation as *sponsor* unless a client uses their own time and money to pay for the coaching.

The question posed earlier "Is it still executive coaching if the organisation does not pay?" may be answered by considering two alternatives: the first would be to delineate executive coaching by who is being coached; the second would be to use the triadic relationship.

An implication of adopting this first distinction is that executive coaching might be considered an expensive niche of life coaching and as one coach rather cynically questioned:

"Is it simply a fancy name that allows coaches to charge more and executives to feel special?"

There would still remain the question: At what level does a manager start to be an executive? Would other fields of coaching for other groups of people or professionals need to be created? Would there be lawyer coaching or doctor coaching?   There are other established types of coaching that describe these dyadic relationships: career coaching, business coaching (suggested for business-owners and entrepreneurs) and life coaching.

The alternative is to use the triadic relationship and this would align with the results from the survey where 60% say *managers at all levels* can receive executive coaching.   In conclusion, and considering the 70% of executive coaches who agree with the triadic definition suggests that the triadic relationship would be a more universally accepted defining characteristic of executive coaching.

Generally executive coaches feel strongly that the relationship between the coach and the executive is highly confidential and if the organisation is too involved in the coaching process then trust and respect are compromised, which would negatively impacts the outcomes.   It is agreed that the coaching content and conversations are private, but some coaches think it is acceptable for the sponsor to see all or part of the action plan and/or high level process.

Many coaches acknowledge the ethical responsibilities and importance of setting clear boundaries within the triadic relationship.   It was suggested that it is the executive's job to share any content from the coaching sessions and as their role exists to better the organisation, they should have more responsibility in translating the benefits of the coaching to the organisation.

Even though the organisation contracts and pays for the executive coaching, their explicit role in the actual coaching program may be limited, as they are "not a voice", but are still present as the context and may have some explicit input during the process at pre-defined points. They ultimately may decide whether their investment was worthwhile.

Coaches acknowledge that the triadic relationship is complicated and it is important to define the confidentially and reporting arrangements during the contracting phase and explicitly agree these with all parties. The coach then works in the service of the executive, but somehow at the same time ensures there is alignment between the executive's and organisational agendas and ensures the coaching is in the context of the organisation's needs. This is a difficult task and can result in conflicts of interest, as one executive coach observes, this is no simple matter:

> "I've seen lots of damage done by other coaches who cannot hold the multiple perspectives simultaneously; a win for the organisation, a win for the executive being coached, a win for that executive's team, customers, etc."

In summary, the nature, complexity and importance of the triadic relationship is what separates executive coaching from other *dyadic* forms of coaching. Although this triadic relationship may occur in other forms of coaching supplied to organisations, it is especially critical when coaching managers and leaders.

"An executive coach acts as a facilitative change-agent working primarily one-to-one with an executive"

The survey shows that 57% of coaches strongly agree and 33% agree with this statement and the qualitative analysis confirms there is fairly universal agreement. Some coaches think there are additional roles that an executive coach can undertake.

In particular, there are themes around increasing the awareness an executive has about themselves and their organisation, gaining increased clarity and thinking together. The role of the coach is described as an "impartial sounding board, awareness trainer and thinking partner". Sperry suggests that this role of confidant and talking partner is one of *executive consultation* describing it as a *sounding board*, but together with the role of *advisor*. (Sperry, 2008)

Another theme emerges around challenging the executive, where one coach describes the role as an "antagonist".

There are a few executive coaches who think that the term *change-agent* implies the coach will be responsible for change, whereas the onus should be on the executive, suggesting that the coach is simply a *catalyst*. However the meaning of *facilitative change-agent* is a person who takes an active role in making the process of change easier, which has a similar meaning to *catalyst*. (The Oxford Dictionary of English (revised edition), 2005)

"An executive coach works in a collaborative equal partnership with an executive"

This statement describes the nature of the relationship between the executive coach and the executive. Overall the quantitative results show strong support for this statement, with 60% strongly agreeing and 30% agreeing. Coaches gave some diverse opinions: a few say it is not equal, others not always equal and one that it isn't even collaborative.

However some executive coaches think that it is equal in terms of respect, but the responsibilities of the two parties are different; the coach owns and supports the process and is there to help or enable the executive to achieve their goals, but the coach should be indifferent to the specific direction or outcome. Overall the executive has more responsibility, does most of the work and ultimately is responsible for translating the benefits of the executive coaching into having an impact on the organisation.

"The purpose of executive coaching is to create sustained change in the Executive's skills, behaviour and performance so that both the executive and their organisation get ultimate benefit"

This statement describes the benefits of executive coaching. The analysis shows this statement has the highest support with 77% of coaches strongly agreeing and 18% agreeing, yet it also has a large amount of the qualitative feedback.

A few executive coaches take this statement to imply that it is they who create the sustained change, as opposed to *the purpose of executive coaching* being to create the sustained change. However, again most suggest that the responsibility lies more with the executive and they only facilitate change or increase its probability.

Some preferred using other words instead of change, such as increasing range, shift or development; emphasising that this is more of what someone has. The word change in this context does encapsulate all of these concepts, but it may be more precise to use the development of skills and performance.

There were a large number of executive coaches who felt there should be a much broader description of the benefits for the executive in particular the concepts of *values, beliefs, identity* and *purpose*. These together with the skills and behaviours already in the definition make up the model of mental processing and organisation called *Neuro-Logical Levels*. (Dilts & DeLozier, 2000)

There are a range of themes regarding the benefit of executive coaching to the organisation. At one end, a couple of executive coaches identify direct bottom-line business benefits and at the other extreme, a few who feel the organisational benefits are secondary or even optional in the process. Many think it is the executive's responsibility to deliver value to the organisation.

A number of executive coaches raise a sensitive but important issue that the executive may choose to leave the organisation as a result of the coaching and although some comment that the organisation might be happy with this result, most realise that this is perhaps not the expected outcome. However some clarify that in the long term the organisation would realise it is better off with another executive who is happier and more motivated in the role.

There are themes throughout highlighting the differences in the roles and responsibilities of each member of the triadic relationship. The issue of confidentiality between the executive coach and executive was considered paramount and that the benefits of executive coaching would flow from the executive and result in value for the organisation.

Summarising the results; executive coaching is for senior managers and leaders in organisations, with more junior managers also often receiving it and occasionally specialists without management responsibility. The definition of executive coaching as *a helping relationship,* although gaining much support does not differentiate it from therapeutic and consulting practices and while a *facilitated learning process* gains the highest support, there were some suggestions that it could be more descriptive and include a new concept of *space.* There is significant agreement with the rest of the definition put forward in the research questions, except for one part regarding *the triadic relationship* that was supported by only 70% of the sample and there was considerable volume of feedback about this from the qualitative data. Together this suggests there is an opportunity to modify the definition so that it would be more universally accepted.

Conclusions

The definition suggested in the research questions was:

> "Executive coaching is a facilitated learning process within a triadic relationship between a professional coach, an executive and their organisation. An executive coach acts as the facilitative change-agent primarily working one-to-one with the executive in a collaborative equal partnership, with a purpose to create sustained

change in the executive's skills, behaviour and performance so that both the executive and their organisation get ultimate benefit."

Hypothesis 1, that 80% of practising executive coaches will agree with the proposed definition, is not proved by this research so the above definition cannot be accepted in full. However only the phrase "within a triadic relationship" failed to gain sufficient agreement to be considered universally acceptable, although still with 70% of the practicing executive coaches agreeing.

Hypothesis 2, that all managers in an organisation can receive executive coaching, is proven. However this distinction may not be universally accepted as only 60% of executive coaches made this distinction.

There are differing opinions whether executive coaching is dyadic, triadic or both and whether it is for all managers or only for senior managers? However with clear majorities, this research concludes that it is triadic and for all managers.

"Executive coaching is for senior managers and leaders in organisations, but more junior managers also often receive it and occasionally specialists without management responsibility."

The nature, complexity and importance of the triadic relationship is what separates executive coaching from other *dyadic* forms of coaching. Although this triadic relationship may occur in other forms of coaching supplied to organisations, it is especially critical when coaching managers and leaders.

It is still possible to find a universally acceptable definition, as there were other reasons the *triadic relationship* was not universally accepted. The main reason given was the rest of the definition failed to make clear the relationships, roles and responsibilities within the triad are different.

Therefore the final conclusion from this research and analysis is that the following definition is more universally acceptable:

> *"Executive coaching is a facilitated learning process within a triadic relationship between a professional <u>executive</u> coach (<u>coach</u>), an executive (<u>client</u>) and their organisation (<u>sponsor</u>).*
>
> *The coach acts as a facilitative change agent, <u>sounding board and challenger</u>; primarily working one-to-one with <u>and in support of</u> the client, in a collaborative equal partnership <u>within a confidential creative space</u>.*
>
> *The <u>goal</u> of executive coaching is to create sustained change in the client's behaviour, skills, <u>beliefs, values, identity, purpose</u> and performance <u>for the benefit of the client and ultimately the triple bottom line of the sponsor</u>."*

The changes from the definition proposed in the research question are underlined. The first change is to use ICF terminology from their code of ethics to make the roles of each party in the triadic relationship and the connection between the definition and ethics clearer. It also has the benefit of making the definition easier to read. (ICF, 2008)

The second change was to add *confidential* into the description of the coach-client partnership, differentiating that relationship further from the others in the triad. Then changes in the flow of the definition make it clearer that the benefit of executive coaching flows from the coach to client to sponsor.

The addition of extra roles for the coach, concepts such as creative space and a broader benefit statement make the definition richer and more universally acceptable.

Finally *purpose* was replaced by *goal* to remove duplicate words. The inclusion of the *triple bottom line* as the ultimate benefit for the sponsor of executive coaching encapsulates current times.

In the introduction, the importance of executive coaching was discussed; its role in ensuring that executives rise to the "modern challenge" and don't just say the right words, but that they take the right action.

The challenge for executive coaching is to move towards a professional status. It's perhaps with some synchronicity that at the same time executive coaching was born so was the *triple bottom line*; coined in the early 1990s, it too is reaching its adult phase. Just recently a company has announced the world's first model to measure corporate sustainability called the *True Sustainability Index*™ that can assess the full *triple bottom line* performance of organisations. (Elkington, 2009; McElroy, 2009)

This delineation and definition of the executive coaching industry must be a key step towards its professional status, and it is proposed that this survey, the largest global executive coaching survey undertaken so far, represents a significant step towards that. This new definition is proposed and recommendations regarding the next steps that future researchers may choose to take are in Chapter 9.

Chapter 5

Why linguistics?

Although we now have a definition of executive coaching, this stilll does not describe in detail what an executive coach does. There are many types of behaviours that an executive coach might undertake, but as will be seen it is the linguistic dimension that is so crucial.

A significant amount, as much as 40% of executive coaching in the US is delivered using primarily language over the telephone, although that trend is currently declining. Some coaches have even concluded that telephone coaching is more effective, however views differ between the sexes; with 17% of males and 34% of females thinking telephone coaching is more effective than face-to-face coaching. (Corbett, 2009)

Carter argues that an effective dialogue is at the heart of good executive coaching and Anderson suggests that in the most mature coaching relationships "coaching flows from a continuous creative conversation." (Anderson, 2005; Carter, 2001)

While the most commonly held view is that language is simply a mechanism for communicating, for the last century scholars of linguistics and philosophy have been putting forward alternative views:

> "Human beings do not live in the objective world alone, nor alone in the world of social activity as ordinarily understood, but are very much at the mercy of the particular language which has become the medium of expression for their society. It is quite an illusion to imagine that one adjusts to reality essentially without the use of

language and that language is merely an incidental means of solving specific problems of communication and reflection. The fact of the matter is that the "real world" is to a large extent unconsciously built up on the language habits of the group." (Sapir, 1929)

Not surprisingly, there is a significant linguistic dimension to Neuro-Linguistic Programming (NLP), which is heavily influenced by Korzybski and his concepts of *mind-body systems* and *humans creating maps of the world*. Language is important because meaning is constructed from words, which in turn affect the emotional state. Korzybski went further and suggested that all progress in human affairs depended upon radical linguistic revision; he gives Einstein's theory of relativity to illustrate how new language had to be created. From Korzybski and others, NLP gave us the pre-supposition that *the map is not the territory*, a key concept that the internal representation we have of the world is not the reality of what is in the world. (Bandler & Grinder, 1975; Harland, 2006; Linder-Pelz & Hall, 2007)

Bandler & Grinder suggest that the way we think and communicate using language includes a process of deleting, distorting and generalising our experiences. They propose the 'META model' that provides practitioners with a tool to transform this impoverished linguistic model of the world and in doing so enable clients to have more choices. Academics studying NLP in a learning context realise our understanding of how these maps are constructed, utilised and changed can be determined from patterns of language. This may hold the key to how learning works. (Tosey & Mathison, 2003)

Since the inception of NLP, many other language models have been suggested, including the 'Milton model', 'sleight of mouth', 'clean language' and 'LAB profile'; yet surprisingly, even in the NLP coaching literature very little has been written about how these tools might be utilised effectively by a coach - let alone an executive coach. (Charvet,

1997; Dilts, 1999; Dove, 2004; Hayes, 2006; Lawley & Tompkins, 2000; McDermott & Jago, 2001; O'Connor & Lages, 2007)

This may be due to a formula that is quoted by many coaches and teachers that downplays the importance of language. The formula comes from Mehrabian's research regarding the influence of words, vocal qualities and facial expressions on how people like a particular communication. His formula is Total Liking = 7% Verbal Liking, + 38% Vocal Liking, + 55% Facial Liking. (Mehrabian, 1981)

These figures are sometimes misused to illustrate that the tone of voice and body language that a coach uses has more impact than words. However Mehrabian himself points out this formula only applies in specific situations:

> "Please note that this and other equations regarding relative importance of verbal and nonverbal messages were derived from experiments dealing with communications of feelings and attitudes (i.e. like-dislike). Unless a communicator is talking about their feelings or attitudes, these equations are not applicable." (Merabian, 2009)

and further analysis shows that the research is flawed in a number of other ways. It is based on two separate experiments combined to create the formula, these experiments only used single words (considered to be an unnatural situation), they did not take into account body language (only fixed facial expressions from photographs) and used only female subjects.

An alternative perspective (and one shared by the author) comes from one of the greatest philosophers of the twentieth century:

> "A main source of our failure to understand is that we do not command a clear view of the use of our words." (Wittgenstein, 1958)

Chapter 6

Linguistic Behaviours

There is no research specifically about the linguistic behaviours of an executive coach and most coaching texts only give them a cursory mention. However there is one model that is presented and is used by a number of training companies.

The figure below (6-1) shows the linguistic model of behaviour called "The Spectrum of Coaching Skills" that describes the range of conversational approaches available to a coach. (Downey, 2003)

Figure 6-1 The spectrum of coaching skills

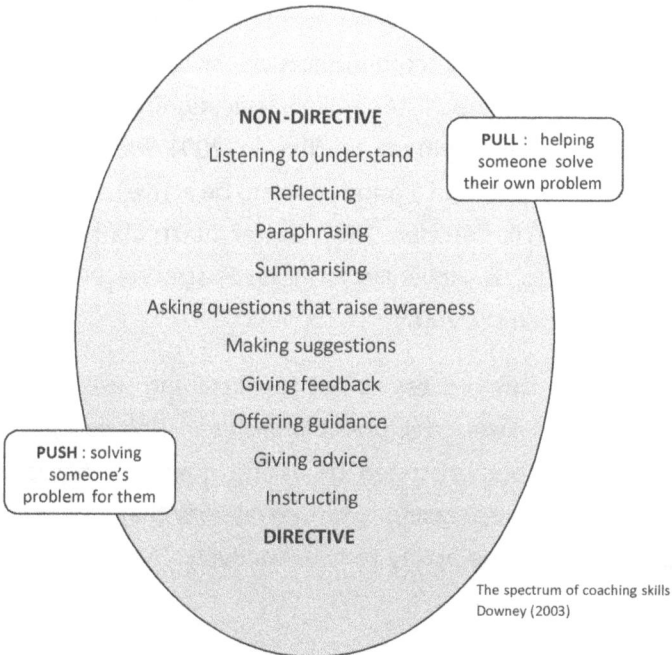

NON-DIRECTIVE

Listening to understand

Reflecting

Paraphrasing

Summarising

Asking questions that raise awareness

Making suggestions

Giving feedback

Offering guidance

Giving advice

Instructing

DIRECTIVE

PULL : helping someone solve their own problem

PUSH : solving someone's problem for them

The spectrum of coaching skills
Downey (2003)

Downey suggests that the magic of coaching occurs at the *non-directive* end of the spectrum, but that directive approaches are still available to a coach and there may be situations where they are applicable. There are others, as we will see, who argue that there are grave dangers in being *directive*.

Listening to Understand

Generally listening is seen as a passive process and not necessarily even a linguistic behaviour. Yet for an executive coach, good listening is seen as an essential quality and the most important linguistic behaviour. Models of listening include levels of listening, active listening and in an ontological approach it plays a pivotal role in coaching. It is even suggested that listening is a key business and life process. (Bresser & Wilson, 2006; Sieler, 2003; Whitmore, 2002)

There has been some qualitative research that points to the importance of listening (and questioning) as the core capabilities of executive coaching. Research found that both executives and their coaches felt that good listening worked best. A survey of UK executives revealed that they are looking for strong communication skills in their coach, more specifically through good listening (and questioning). Another survey by the Institute of Employment Studies in 2001 found that executives described the core skills of a good coach to be active listening (and asking probing questions). (Altman, 2007; Carter, 2001; Clarke & Dembkowski, 2006; Hall, Otazo, & Hollenbeck, 1999; Passmore, 2006; Passmore & Gibbes, 2007; Sparrow, 2007)

Baker describes this process as not just listening well but listening for themes, patterns, strengths, possibilities, etc. Bolt suggests that deep listening can be demonstrated by asking questions based on what is heard or using paraphrasing. Bartlett asserts that the greatest skill a coach can bring is the ability to listen actively. A best practice coach is able to listen with nuance and sensitivity. (Baker, 2005; Bartlett, 2005; Bolt, 2005; Morgan, Harkins, & Goldsmith, 2005)

The importance of listening is clear when you consider a concept that *the meaning of what is spoken is what is received.* This pre-supposition forms the basis of some linguistic approaches to coaching, including NLP and Ontological. (Dilts & DeLozier, 2000; Sieler, 2003)

The summary seems to be that listening is the most important linguistic skill an executive coach can possess.

Reflecting, Paraphrasing and Summarising

These linguistic behaviours have been collectively grouped together as they involve taking what the executive has said and repeating it back to them, with varying amounts of change. The words *clarifying* or *clarity* are sometimes used to indicate that one purpose for these behaviours is to help the executive gain more insight to their own thought processes. Hedman also observes that these linguistic behaviours are the output side of *Active Listening* and Bresser & Wilson suggest they are key skills for a coach. (Bresser & Wilson, 2006; Hedman, 2001)

Reflecting (also called repeating, repetition and restatement) involves using the exact words of the executive and therefore has the least change. Downey says it does not show understanding but still may be useful when the words have particular significance to the executive; while Hedman says it clarifies, demonstrates interest and implies respect for the executive. The *Clean Language* model insists that a coach is careful not only to make use of a client's exact words, but also their way of speaking these words. (Lawley & Tompkins, 2000)

Summarising is tying several statements together into a theme to check for accuracy of meaning and according to Downey does demonstrate understanding.

Paraphrasing involves the most changes, using different words to repeat back what the executive has said. Downey suggests that a coach uses words they believe are a better way of expressing what a client means, while Hedman suggests that a coach should emphasise and explore important aspects of a client's words.

There are mixed views on the purpose and usefulness of these three clarifying behaviours. Whitmore suggests reflecting and summarising are key skills for a coach. So while paraphrasing is also useful, it is important for a coach to remain within a client's world and keep their *MAP (metaphors, assumptions and pre-suppositions)* out of the process. (Lawley & Tomkins, 2004; Whitmore, 2002)

In summary these are useful tools for an executive coach, but care needs to be taken when using paraphrasing.

Asking Questions that Raise Awareness

It can be seen that questioning is about much more than just raising awareness. Adams and Marquardt present two different perspectives on the reasons and benefits of asking questions and the table below (2-1)

Table 6-2 The broader applications of questioning

Adams Top 12 Reasons	Marquardt 10 Benefits
• Gather information • Build and maintain relationships • Learn, teach, and reflect • Think clearly, critically, and strategically • Challenge assumptions • Solve problems and make decisions • Clarify and confirm listening • Negotiate and resolve conflicts • Set and accomplish goals • Take charge and focus attention • Create and innovate – open new possibilities • Catalyze productive and accountable thinking, conversation and action	• Cause a person to focus and stretch • Create deep reflection • Challenge taken for granted assumptions that prevent people from acting in new and forceful ways • Generate courage and strength • Lead to breakthrough thinking • Contain the keys that open the door to great solutions. • Enable people to better view the situation. • Open doors in the mind and get people to think more deeply • Test assumptions and cause individuals to explore why they act in the way that they do as well as why they choose to take action. • Generate positive and powerful action

shows these broader applications of questioning. (Adams, 2008; Marquardt, 2005)

Questions can be more or less directive depending on their purpose and how they are structured. For example leading or Socratic questions might be structured based on the questioner already thinking they know the answer, versus clean questions which have no pre-suppositions and totally exist in the client's world.   (Carey & Mullan, 2004; Lawley & Tompkins, 2000)

Although questioning is cited as a key competency by the accrediting bodies (such as the ICF), mentioned as an important skill in the same surveys cited before (in listening) and at the heart of both the GROW coaching and NLP linguistic models; it is remarkably difficult to find practicing coaches who say much about it. Baker is called the "queen of powerful questions" yet says more about listening. Overall there is much less written than might be expected. (Bresser & Wilson, 2006; Charvet, 1997; Hayes, 2006; Lawley & Tomkins, 2006; Whitmore, 2002)

However some practitioners who do refer to questioning tend to suggest that it is a *core* competency of executive coaching. (Altman, 2007; Clarke & Dembkowski, 2006; Helgesen, 2005; Sparrow, 2007)

Stoltzfus suggests that questioning is synonymous with coaching and suggests that when you ask questions you also start listening. The act of asking questions moves the asker away from being an *expert*, from mentoring, consulting or advising, towards being a coach. Whilst others observe that having a curious approach is the key to being a great coach, using this to ask penetrating questions. (Sherman & Freas, 2004; Stoltzfus, 2008)

Goldberg proposes a model of questioning for coaches called *Question Centred Therapy*, that fills a perceived gap between the importance of questioning and the lack of any systematic methods. Goldberg claims that "most coaches would agree that coaching can be up to 85% questioning", citing the lack of systematic training or books as limiting a coach's capability.   A concept from her model of the *Learner-Judger Mindset* was later integrated with approaches from appreciative inquiry. (Goldberg-Adams, Schiller, & Cooperrider, 2004; Goldberg, 1998, 1999)

Appreciative (Inquiry) Coaching has evolved from this consultative (organisational development) world of appreciative inquiry and also places questioning at the heart of coaching, but not just any questions, the right questions.   Appreciative Coaching questions are not only positively framed, as they would be for an NLP coach using well-formed outcomes, but "questions that are carefully crafted to create a joyful, focused state of mind as the client considers and answers them." (Gordon, 2008; Hayes, 2006; Orem, Binkert, & Clancy, 2007)

The challenge for a best practice executive coach is to ask penetrating questions that take the executive places they never would have got to on their own, despite the fact that the executive has more knowledge and experience in their role than their coach. (Morgan et al., 2005)

The summary seems to be that questioning may also be the most important skill for an executive coach to possess.

Directive or Non-directive Behaviour

Downey is reluctant to spend a whole chapter discussing the remaining more directional behaviours. He observes that in his own practice he spends over 80% at the non-directive end of the spectrum, claiming it's more effective. He suggests the dangers of a directional approach are they remove responsibility and choice from the executive.

So at this half-way point in Downey's model, it is worth reflecting on the debate that is rumbling on in the coaching world. In a very recent paper that explored conflicting paradigms in coaching, nine approaches were analysed. The conclusion was that humanistic, systemic, adult learning and goal orientated approaches were non-directive, while behaviourist, adult development, cognitive, positive psychology and adventure approaches were directive. (Ives, 2008)

Ives' analysis seems at odds with the literature that has almost no references to linguistic behaviours that are more directional. His evidence for a directive approach seems to have come from just two sources. However his analysis confirms that all the approaches are reliant on the non-directional skills of listening and questioning. He concludes by posing a question, that he claims will provoke intense disagreement and polarise opinion: *"Does a coach only 'ask' or may s/he also 'tell'?"* This research would like to answer that question.

Giving Feedback

Research conducted in the US interviewed 75 executives and 15 executive coaches to determine what works best and least well in executive coaching and indicated that while both agreed *good listening* and *being a sounding board* were important. In terms of linguistic skills the coaches mentioned *reflecting*; while executives cited *making suggestions* and *giving feedback*. (Hall et al., 1999)

These executives value straight, honest, realistic and challenging feedback but felt that receiving all negative or anything *touchy-feely* (dealing with others' feelings, not results) works least well. Overall they feel that providing all feedback with no ideas worked less well. One could argue that these are quite arbitrary distinctions; what might be *touchy feely* or *negative* for one executive, might be *results* or *positive* for another. This is just one of the challenges that executive coaches have when taking a more directional approach.

Carter suggests that along with the more non-directive methods, feedback is an important skill for an executive coach. Kouzes cited John Gardner who said "Pity the leader caught between unloving critics and uncritical lovers" and concluded that what leaders need are *loving critics*.

Barnes suggests that a challenge for a successful executive coach is not to be afraid to confront leaders with difficult feedback. (Barnes, 2005; Carter, 2001; Kouzes, 2005)

Often when the literature talks about feedback it is referring to feedback coming from the organisation. For example, from a performance review with an executive's boss or sponsor; a 360 degree report from bosses, piers, reports and others; or the coach may have collected specific data about an executive from particular stakeholders.

This feedback may also come more directly from the coach from the interpretation of a self-assessment tool or from observations of the executive either in the coaching sessions or at work.

The process of feedback is a central element of the coaching process. An executive coach needs to be aware of the feedback orientation of both the executive and the organisation. Gregory et al. suggests that the *Feedback Orientation Scale* and *Feedback Environment Scale* could provide researchers and coaches with useful tools to measure these. Research shows that an executive's openness to receiving feedback is a factor in building a close and trusting coaching relationship and that openness to feedback (together with follow up) is a major contributor to being a more effective leader. (Alvey & Barclay, 2007; Goldsmith, 2002; Gregory, Levy, & Jeffers, 2008; Joo, 2005)

An executive coach may use many linguistic behaviours to deliver feedback, particularly when it's from the organisation or self-assessment tools. A coach may use questions, reflection, summarising and paraphrasing to help executives unravel and get the maximum value from these types of feedback.

However when the feedback is based on the coach's own judgments it has been suggested that a coach must be seen as an effective source and be "credible, trustworthy and exhibit some degree of expertise." (Gregory et al., 2008)

In summary, the literature suggests feedback is an important skill for an executive coach.

Making Suggestions (Providing Ideas)

Downey defines suggestions as meaning "ideas that the coach believes are appropriate in the situation". He warns that care is needed when presenting these ideas, to ensure that the client has a free choice whether or not to accept them.

However the dictionary suggests alternative definitions of the words that significantly change the meaning: *making* can also signify compelling the client to accept an idea and *suggestion* can mean indicating a fact. Both of these meanings conflict with the concept that the client has free choice to accept or reject the idea. As the label *providing ideas* is synonymous with *making suggestions* but without these connotations, it is used in this research. (The Oxford Dictionary of English (revised edition), 2005)

As part of the option phase of the GROW model, Whitmore suggests that coaches can ensure they avoid any pitfalls by providing ideas for options, but only when the executive has exhausted their own possibilities, ensuring that the coach's ideas are not given more priority than the executives. (Whitmore, 2002)

Hall observes that executives value *good action ideas or pointers*, but are much less impressed with *self-serving, naive or unrealistic ones*. It seems an arbitrary distinction what might constitute an *unrealistic* or *naive* idea and a coach needs to be careful when choosing which ideas to share. (Hall et al., 1999)

In summary *providing ideas* may be a useful behaviour for an executive coach providing those ideas are acceptable to the executive.

Giving Advice

Downey has problems using this behaviour during a coaching session and suggests that a coach who has reverted to *giving advice* has not paid attention to the coaching process.

Giving advice is one of the behaviours that might be expected from a consultant or mentor and the actual word *advisor* is sometimes used as a synonym for consultant. (Bresser & Wilson, 2006; Feldman & Lankau, 2005)

One editor describes the 50 US based executive coaches who contributed to their publication as *world class advisors* who could be called coaches and consultants, although the book focuses on their work as coaches. (Morgan et al., 2005)

Even if a coach is aware that executive coaching is facilitative rather than telling and that the magic occurs when being non-directive rather than directive, they may still fall into the trap of giving advice. They may be lured there by an executive who does not understand the coaching role or process and may initially appreciate some good advice. However, as shown in the case of feedback, it is easy to provide something of dubious value to the executive that could have a detrimental effect on the credibility and ultimately trust in the coach. (Bluckert, 2005)

In conclusion, giving advice is not a useful behaviour for an executive coach, although there may be those who have a different opinion based on either their location or background.

Offering Guidance

Downey does not differentiate between *offering guidance* and *giving advice* in his text and the dictionary suggests they may be synonymous.

Offering guidance is the presentation of something that will solve problems, which can be either accepted or rejected as desired. *Giving advice* means the putting forward of information for future prudent action. However *giving* has a much stronger inference that what is being put forward is to be accepted. (The Oxford Dictionary of English (revised edition), 2005)

Stern suggests an executive coach needs to provide "specific guidance on how the executive should behave and communicate." It is interesting that the same author then refers to a coach as a consultant and has a consulting background. (Stern, 2004)

A recent review of the coaching industry proposes that it has become more non-directive as it has matured. However Ives also contends that the pendulum is returning to being more directive again with growth in therapeutic coaching, resulting in "a partial return towards guidance". (Ives, 2008)

In summary offering guidance is not a useful behaviour for an executive coach, but there may be those who have a different opinion based on either their background or years of experience.

Instructing

The most directive of the behaviours according to Downey's model is *instructing*, that he claims is sometimes appropriate to use in a coaching session. To see how this might be misunderstood it is worth looking at the definition of these verbs: to instruct, to direct and to tell.

All three words have meanings that imply strong directive action, in the sense of ordering someone to do something or act in a certain way. However they also have less directive meanings – telling means simply to communicate, directing means showing someone how to get somewhere and instructing simply means teaching someone a subject or skill. (The Oxford Dictionary of English (revised edition), 2005)

In his text, Downey appears to be referring to teaching, where the coach is imparting a technique or approach that the coach knows but the coachee does not. However his views seem to be based on his experiences as a tennis coach and he does talk about telling in other coaching sessions but says it was always a mistake. He warns of the dangers of telling that could lead to coachees becoming dependant on the coach.

This illustrates the importance of words, boundaries and definitions and how they are used. A coach that teaches can either acknowledge that they are teaching or can choose to categorise teaching behaviours as coaching ones.

There are no practitioners or researchers that suggest telling or instructing are relevant behaviours for an executive coach.

In summary there seems enough of a distinction between telling and instructing to include both in the survey, but it seems from the literature that neither are relevant behaviours for an executive coach.

Being a role model and *explaining* are two other linguistic behaviours that are not in Downey's model but mentioned in the literature.

Being a Role Model

The concept of *being a role model* is one from the mentoring world that is often used to describe how a mentor can be seen as a positive example to the mentee. (Clutterbuck & Lane, 2004)

How could this translate into the coaching world and how does it relate to linguistic behaviours? Stern mentions *being a role model* as a key skill for an executive coach without specifically putting it in a language context. (Stern, 2004)

It is possible to use linguistic techniques to re-frame the language of a client, for example using *sleight of mouth*. Executives may start to ask questions of their team using techniques that are a significant part of the coaching sessions, without any formal instruction or teaching. These interventions would sit in a linguistic category of "being a role model". (Dilts, 1999)

In conclusion, it will be interested to see how other practitioners view *being a role model* in the context of linguistic behaviour.

Explaining

Explaining is a core skill that some executives say they look for in a great executive coach. (Carter, 2001)

Explaining is to "make (an idea or situation) clear to someone by describing it in more detail or revealing relevant facts" and seems distinct enough from other behaviours to include in the survey. (The Oxford Dictionary of English (revised edition), 2005)

Summary

Based on the anecdotal, theoretical and limited research evidence available for this literature review it could be hypothesised that listening, questioning and the clarifying skills of reflecting, summarising and paraphrasing are the core linguistic behaviours used by an executive coach.

This research will now seek verification of this with more valid methods and methodology.

However when it comes to the more directive behaviours, things are a little more confusing and it is not clear how explaining, feedback and being a role model might be used linguistically by an executive coach. There is some uncertainty about how the most directive behaviours such as telling, giving advice, instructing, offering guidance and providing ideas may be viewed.

There are also suggestions that the location, background and experience of an executive coach may be a factor in how directive they are.

Research Questions and Hypotheses

What is the relevance and use of different linguistic behaviours by an executive coach practicing executive coaching in the English language?

Hypothesis 3 is that a coach spends more time listening than speaking in the practice of executive coaching in the English language.

Hypothesis 4 is that the non-directive linguistic behaviours of listening, questioning, reflecting, summarising and paraphrasing are the most relevant and used in the practice of executive coaching in the English language.

Hypothesis 5 is that the linguistic behaviours of being a role model and feedback are relevant and used in the practice of executive coaching in the English language.

Hypothesis 6 is that the directive linguistic behaviours of telling, instructing, giving advice, providing ideas, offering guidance and explaining are not relevant or used in the practice of executive coaching in the English language.

Hypothesis 7 is that the relevance and use of directive linguistic behaviours of telling, instructing, giving advice, providing ideas, offering guidance and explaining are determined by the location (7a), background (7b) and experience (7c) of an executive coach.

The detailed results and analysis for hypothesis 7 can be found in Chapter 7. The final answers and conclusions for each of these hypotheses can be found in Chapter 8.

Results and Analysis

Time Executive Coaches Spend Listening vs speaking

The chart below (6-3) and the table over the page (6-4) show that on average executive coaches spend much more time listening. However there are a small number of coaches that listen for less than half the time (27 cases) or speak for more than half the time (22 cases).

The qualitative data from 604 cases showed that many executive coaches were eager to provide further distinctions within the category of speaking, in particular to separate questioning from speaking. A number of cases described *other* as non-linguistic behaviours such as thinking, observing, note taking and using somatic processes. The most frequently

Chart 6-3 Time executive coaches spend listening vs speaking

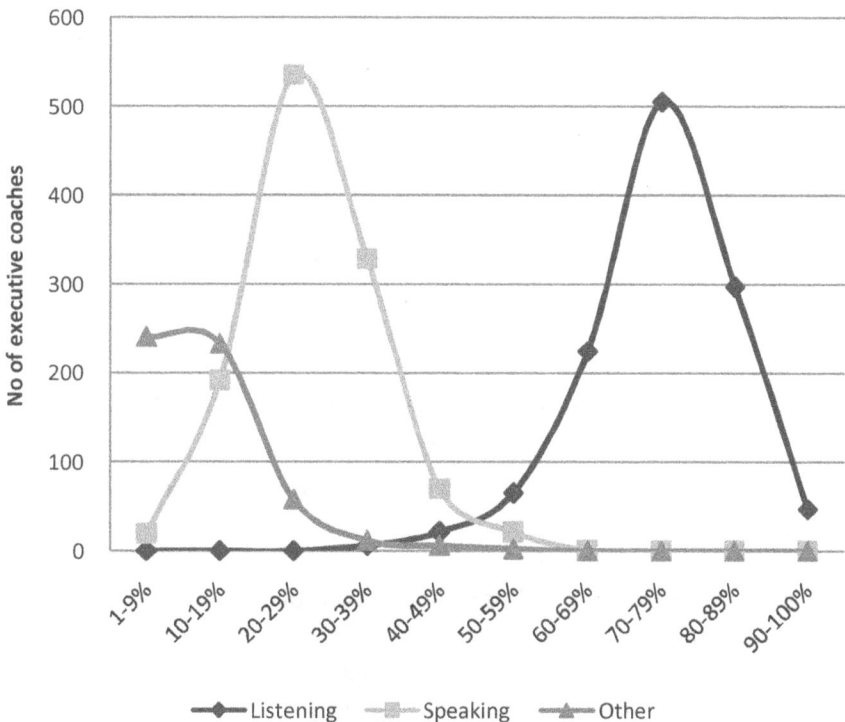

Table 6-4 Time a executive coach spend listening vs speaking

	Listening Time %	Speaking Time %	Other Time %
N	1166	1166	1165
Mean	70.98%	24.34%	4.68%
99% Confidence Interval for Mean:			
Lower Bound	70.22%	23.65%	4.15%
Upper Bound	71.79%	24.97%	5.21%
Standard Deviation	10.400	8.774	7.049
Median	70%	25%	0%
Mode	70%	20%	0%

occurring descriptive that could be considered a linguistic behaviour was *silence*.

Silence is "the centre of power in conversation" and "holding the space for awareness"; being silent isn't a passive act but a critical, albeit small, piece of the linguistic makeup. Although just over half of the sample answered zero for *other time*, about 5% may also have included silent time as listening. Practitioners have recently begun to suggest that silence could be an important linguistic behaviour for an executive coach. (Angus, 2008; Leedham, 2008)

Two executive coaches identified "laughing" as a distinct behaviour. It would be interesting to see if there are other linguistic but non-verbal behaviours that play, an important yet unconscious role in executive coaching.

In summary, executive coaches do spend considerably more of their time listening to their clients.

The Relevance of Linguistic Behaviours

The chart below (6-5) is interpreted by looking at the depth of blackness; the greater the area of darkness, the greater the relevance of the linguistic behaviour. In order to make the chart easy to read it has also been sorted in order of most relevance from left to right (based on the mean score).

Chart 6-5 Ratings of the relevance of linguistic behaviours

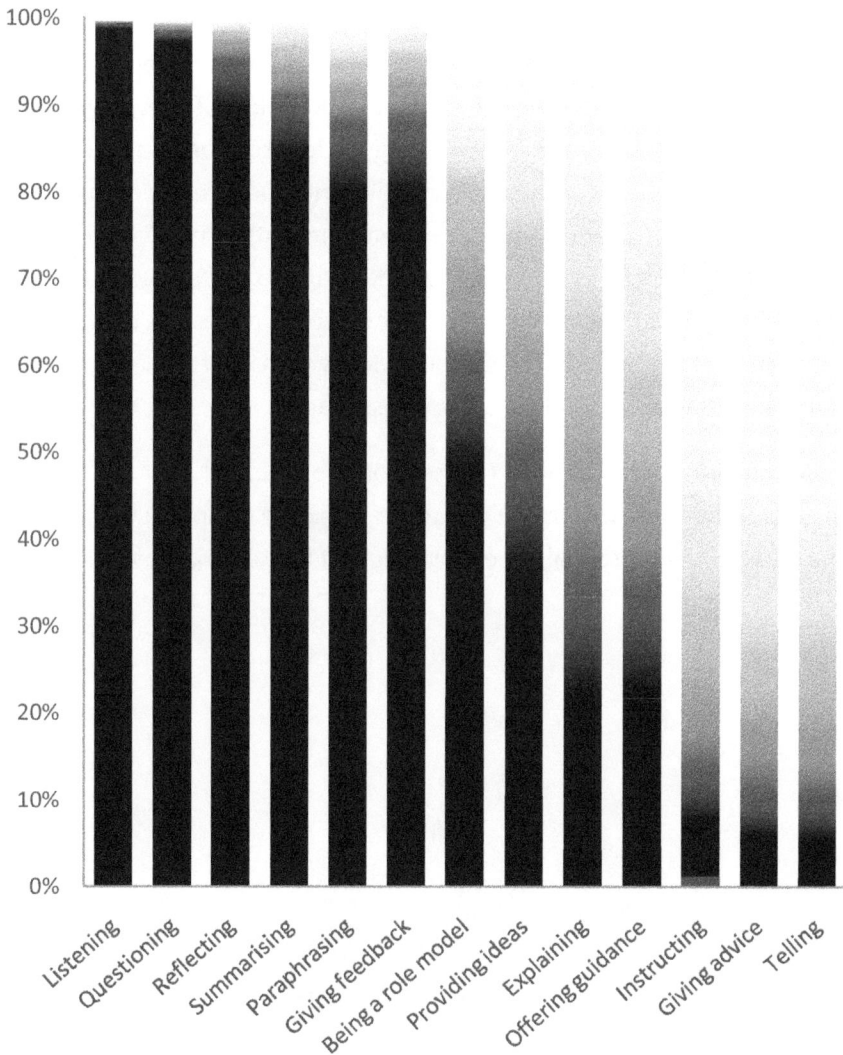

The chart shows there is almost complete agreement that *listening* and *questioning* are totally relevant. *Reflecting, summarising* and *paraphrasing* are the three behaviours that were identified in the literature review as being related because they all involve processing and responding directly to what the executive says. It is interesting that the most relevant of these (*reflecting*) involves no changes to the words spoken, whilst the least relevant (*paraphrasing*) involves the most changes. *Giving feedback* has an almost identical profile to *paraphrasing*. *Being a role model* received the most distributed scores (confirmed by the standard deviation in Table 6-6) that may have been caused by uncertainties about what this involves linguistically. The next grouping of *providing ideas, explaining* and *offering guidance* were given less support, but still had a majority of executive coaches giving a relevant score greater than 5 (on a scale of 1 to 10 where 10 is completely relevant). The least relevant linguistic behaviours for an executive coach are *instructing, giving advice* and *telling*. It is worth noting that the scores for these three differ significantly from the rest of the behaviours with over 80% of coaches rating less than 5 and over 50% rating less than 2 .

The results logically fall into five sets of linguistic behaviours that are illustrated by the background colours in the table opposite (6-9), where the darker shades highlight the most relevant linguistic behaviour.

Table 6-6 Ratings of the relevance of linguistic behaviours

	N	Mean	99% Confidence Interval for Mean:		Standard Deviation	Median	Mode
			Lower Bound	Upper Bound			
Listening	1173	9.82	9.76	9.87	0.766	10	10
Questioning	1173	9.64	9.56	9.71	0.993	10	10
Reflecting	1173	9.06	8.95	9.17	1.432	10	10
Summarising	1173	8.75	8.62	8.88	1.738	9	10
Paraphrasing	1173	8.55	8.4	8.7	1.973	9	10
Giving feedback	1172	8.55	8.41	8.69	1.871	9	10
Being a role model	1172	6.78	6.57	6.98	2.712	7	10
Providing ideas	1173	6.11	5.92	6.3	2.551	6	8
Explaining	1173	5.3	5.13	5.49	2.382	5	5
Offering guidance	1173	5.06	4.87	5.26	2.573	5	3
Instructing	1173	3.41	3.24	3.59	2.298	3	1
Giving advice	1173	3.17	3.01	3.33	2.16	3	1
Telling	1173	3.08	2.92	3.24	2.176	2	1

In summary, the least directive activities received the highest ratings for relevance and the most directive received the lowest ratings. The exception is questioning that receives almost the highest rating despite being considered by Downey as more directive than paraphrasing.

The use of linguistic speaking behaviours

The chart below (6-7) is interpreted by looking at the depth of blackness; the greater the area of darkness, the more a particular linguistic behaviour is used. In order to make the chart easy to read it has also been sorted in order of most used from left to right (based on the mean score).

This chart shows that the pattern of the usage of linguistic behaviours follows a similar profile to that of the relevance. *Questioning* was clearly

Chart 6-7 Which linguistic speaking behaviours are used the most?

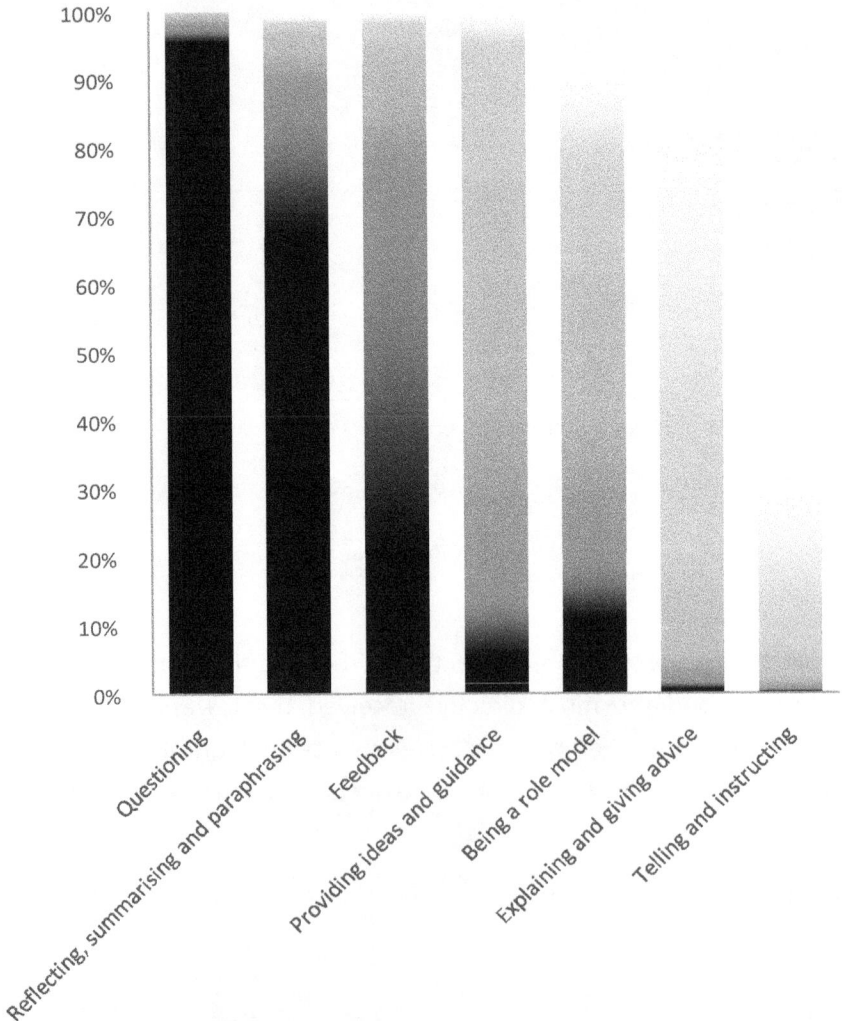

ranked as the most used linguistic input from a coach, with over 95% ranking it first or second. Over 90% ranked *telling and instructing* either last or next to last.

The chart below (6-8) shows that *being a role model* provided the most disparate results and had a lower ranking for usage than might have been expected from the relevance profile.

Chart 6-8 Which speaking behaviours are used the most

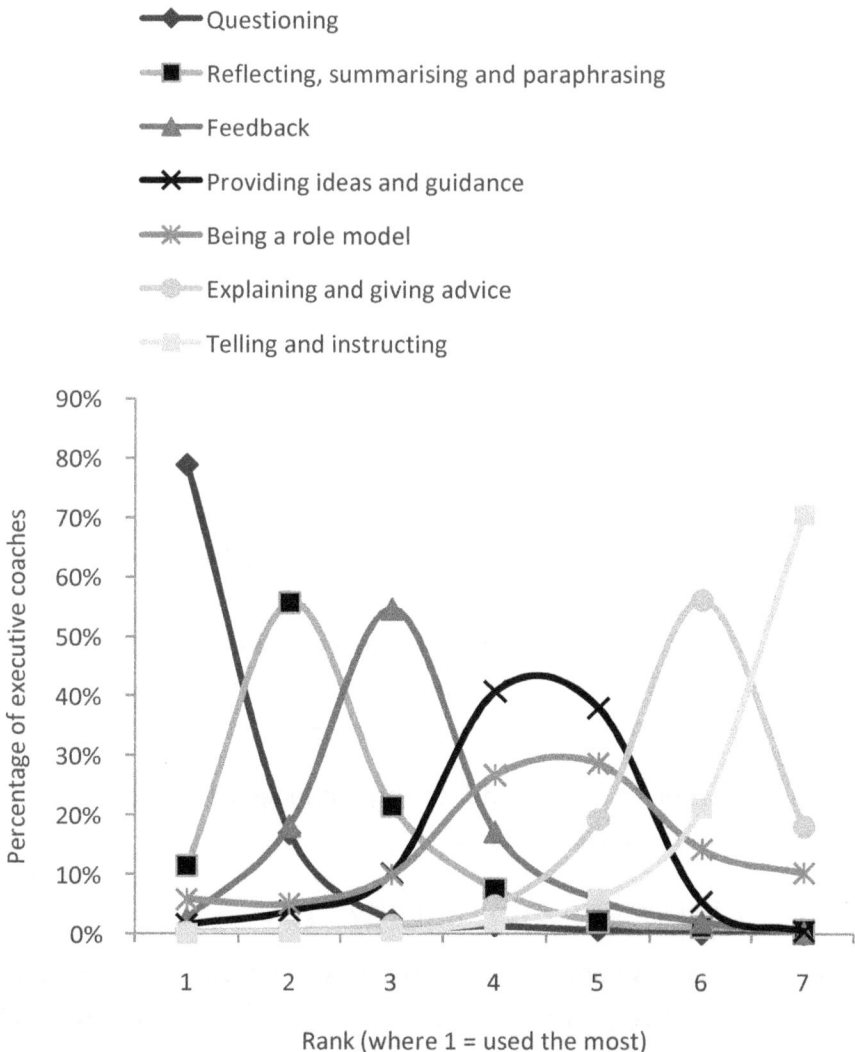

Rank (where 1 = used the most)

Linguistic Behaviours

The qualitative analysis is primarily organised in the sets of linguistic behaviours highlighted earlier and analyses any new themes that are suggested by the 450 executive coaches, who in total gave over 6,000 words of feedback about other linguistic behaviours.

Listening and Questioning

The qualitative data confirms the results of the quantitative analysis, executive coaches say *listening* is the "non negotiable key to success" and together with *questioning* is what coaching is all about. There is also a distinction between listening for what is said and listening for what is not said, i.e. being aware of non-verbal clues, moods and the "big picture".

Questioning is such a versatile linguistic behaviour; one coach even suggests that "ideas and advice can be evoked from the client using them", which as Carey & Mullan observe is a very Socratic approach. However most coaches prefer to use clean, powerful and open questions: some referring to them as inquiring, requesting, asking, enquiring, wondering or simply being curious. (Carey & Mullan, 2007)

Questioning is a very powerful tool and some coaches may not even realise the extent to which they use it. One executive coach provided three new categories of behaviour: clarifying, challenging and sourcing; then proceeded to give three linguistic examples that were all questions: "What does that really mean?", "Do you really believe that?" and "What's behind that statement?"

In conclusion questioning and listening are indeed the core linguistic behaviours of executive coaching.

Reflecting, Summarising and Paraphrasing

Executive coaches confirm that *reflecting* is the most potent of these techniques, although some use other words, such as *mirroring* and *clarifying* to describe the same behaviour. It was interesting to note that both of these words were used by other coaches in contexts, with quite difference meanings: *mirroring* in terms of physical matching and *clarifying* questions .

There are comments that *summarising and paraphrasing* require more interpretation from the coach. In particular the use of *paraphrasing* comes with some risks attached namely that using the coach's words might lose the client. However there are some potential benefits as this can also provide valuable alternative perspectives and this is often referred to as *reframing*.

Giving Feedback

The dictionary defines *giving feedback* as "evaluative information about an action, event or process given to the original source". (Merriam-Webster, 2009)

The descriptions provided by executive coaches for *giving feedback* fall into the three primary representational systems (visual, audio and kinaesthetic) of the coach and these are described as *offering observations*, *straight talking* and *intuiting* respectively. Therefore *giving feedback* is based on the evaluation and judgment of the coach and some make this explicit when they say "tell the truth as we see it", "provide reality checks" or "letting them know when they are kidding themselves". As giving feedback involves a judgmental process, some coaches seek explicit permission to give it, while others focus on giving positive feedback.

The data suggests the line between the definitions of *giving feedback* and *reflecting, summarising and paraphrasing* may have been a fine one for some coaches. One coach describes *"reflecting* back what you hear, see and experience". However *reflecting* back what you see or experience is actually *feedback,* because when you convert from one representational system to another, you evaluate and put your experiences into your own map and then words.

Giving feedback may also come in the form of providing *distinctions*. A coach may identify names, i.e. define terminology and speech acts in the language an executive is using that allows for more distinctions; these concepts come from linguistic theory of speech acts that is an integral part of Ontological Coaching. (Sieler, 2003)

In conclusion, feedback is a broad ranging and important linguistic behaviour for an executive coach to master.

Being a role model

The descriptions regarding *being a role model* confirm what is suggest by the quantitative analysis that there are a wide range of opinions and some confusion about the meaning in the context of linguistic behaviour. Therefore It is concluded that the term does not represent a linguistic behaviour but is a way of delivering linguistic behaviours, such that an executive may model and learn the behaviours themselves.

Providing Ideas, Explaining and Offering Guidance

Executive coaches suggest a number of alternatives to the word *ideas* that are being provided such as "critical thinking insight", "concrete examples", "new ideas", "pragmatic wisdom", "suggestions", "possibilities", "hypotheses" and "concepts". All these are ideas coming from the coach's world and perspective and therefore adequately described by *providing ideas*. Coaches describe *explaining* in a similar way to *providing ideas* and one coach grouped these together with *offering guidance,* describing all three as the intention to "broaden the thinking" of the executive, but they never "constitute recommendations". Another comment about *offering guidance* was that it shouldn't be undertaken by a coach.

Instructing, Giving Advice and Telling

Some executive coaches use the more non-directional meanings of *instructing* and *telling* in their comments. *Instructing* as in educating or sharing knowledge; *telling* as in telling a story or a joke! Most coaches were clear that these behaviours were not suitable for executive coaching; *giving advice* is for consulting. However one coach felt it may be acceptable with the executives permission and with an understanding it is not to direct.

Another executive coach observed that:

> "all the language behaviours above are relevant when used appropriately and with mastery in executive coaching conversation and process. For example, there is a time to instruct 'just take a deep breath now before you answer the question'".

On the one hand this could show that as a coach becomes more experienced and masterly they may use more directive behaviours effectively or on the other hand it could be a justification for calling consulting, executive coaching.

New linguistic behaviours

Although the question in the survey asked for other linguistic behaviours, half of the data fell into categories already rated. This illustrates the complexity of this topic and the way different people around the world may use different terminology to describe the same concept. The concepts presented below were either sufficiently distinct or very prevalent in the data to warrant more in depth discussion whether they do in fact represent new categories:

Silence

The concept of silence, space, pauses or as one coach put it "non-language time" has already been identified earlier in this chapter as an important dimension in executive coaching.

Acknowledging

There are a number of themes grouped together under this description, the most popular being acknowledging.

The descriptions, in order of popularity, are acknowledging, encouraging, empathising, supporting, affirming, championing, celebrating, cheerleading, inspiring, praising, validating, etc. All could be individually considered as a form of feedback and are positive, and together they represent a view that they are distinct and important enough to be considered a separate category.

This type of behaviour has been described in 'Transactional Analysis' as *positive strokes*. Positive strokes are "units of interpersonal recognition that people need to survive and thrive", Steiner described them as "warm fuzzies". (ITAA, 2009; Steiner, 1969)

Although the meanings of these descriptions are different, it is concluded that the definition of acknowledging as "recognising the importance or quality of" provided the best description of what is happening linguistically. And although this may be a form of positive feedback, it is concluded that in the context of executive coaching it may be considered a distinct linguistic behaviour.

Challenging

Challenging was the most common description in the data, with only a couple of other distinctions, "playing devil's advocate" and "confronting". However it is not clear whether it is a separate linguistic behaviour, some executive coaches say it is a form of questioning with more focused intent or more than pure questioning, although still implying *questioning*.

Challenging may not just be about questioning, but might apply to any linguistic behaviour, for example: challenging feedback, reflecting in a challenging tone and clearly any directive activity could be extremely challenging depending on the executive's perspective.   A few examples expand on the concept of *challenging*: "to try new behaviours", "to step out of the comfort zone", "the executive's assessments and assumptions", "their language" and as one coach so eloquently puts it, "their BS". However none of these descriptions suggest a distinct linguistic behaviour.

In conclusion, challenging is a characteristic of other linguistic behaviours and in particular asking challenging questions and giving challenging feedback that are important dimensions of those respective linguistic behaviours.

Brainstorming

Brainstorming is mentioned by a few coaches, one commenting that it is *providing ideas* another saying it's opposed to *providing ideas*. Other coaches suggests a similar concept of strategising that is more of a joint collaboration than *providing ideas*, *giving advice* or *telling*.

The descriptive information leads to the conclusion that this is not a linguistic behaviour but a process of co-creation or drawing out an executive's ideas using *questioning* and *providing ideas* together with more directive input from the coach.

If the executive coach is a full participant in the brainstorm, as opposed to a facilitator, then is consulting really taking place?

Non-verbal language

This theme of *non-verbal language* includes one executive coach who laughs with his or her clients. A few others mention important sounds and noises that *acknowledge*, *affirm* and *encourage* the executive. These sounds and noises are sometimes referred to as natural exclamations like mmm, er, *ah,* ooo, etc. that may be a key way that coaches demonstrate active listening, give feedback and ask questions. For many coaches these behaviours may be taking place unconsciously. In conducting the trial for this survey recordings were made of interviews with executive coaches and in the following transcript, the last *mmm* (in bold) is used by the coach as a reflecting behaviour:

> "in terms of language I am not an auditory person mmm at least that's not my mmm that's not my prime perceptionary mmm sense *mmm* I'm visual"

In conclusion this non-verbal language may be simply a part of other linguistic behaviours such as questioning, reflection and feedback.

Sharing stories

Many executive coaches talk about using metaphors; however it is not always clear whether they are referring to storytelling or using metaphoric language. Included in the storytelling group are those who read poetry, recount their own life story or share their own experiences; as well as those that tell stories. This seems to be sufficiently distinct from other behaviours. The potential value to executive coaches of *sharing stories* is illustrated by Owen's 58 ways stories can be used and Dunbar's text specifically written for coaches. (Dunbar, 2005; Owen, 2001)

Other Linguistic Skills

A small number of themes from the analysis are important skills that a coach might use with any of the linguistic behaviours. These are using the sub-modalities of language, in particular *tone, pace* and - a personal favourite word in this whole book - ***cadence*** that means *lilt* and *tempo*; using *humour* with the concepts of *lightness* and *fun*; using language that is non-judgmental; using metaphoric language including analogies; and using a language of *future* and *possibility*.

Coaches comment that executive coaches should speak in a concise way using the themes and patterns of the executive's language, not interrupting or cutting them off!

Summary

Executive coaches do spend considerably more of their time listening to their clients. Other than speaking, silence is also a factor in the linguistic makeup of executive coaching.

Within speaking, it is the least directive activities that get the highest ratings for both relevance and use.

These behaviours neatly fall into a number of sets that together with the qualitative feedback on what other speaking behaviours may be relevant in executive coaching suggest that *being a role model* is not a linguistic behaviour, but that *silence, acknowledging* and *sharing stories* are distinct enough to be included in a new model of linguistic behaviour that will be presented in Chapter 8.

Chapter 7

Demographic Analysis of Linguistic Behaviour

This chapter analyses linguistic behaviour and searches for any statistically significant differences in these results when they are grouped demographically by location, background and experience.

Warning: this chapter is full of in depth statistical analysis and those who wish to by-pass can turn to the end of the chapter for a summary!

Listening versus speaking

The charts below and on the following page (7-1, 7-2 and 7-3) suggests that on average executive coaches who live in the US or from an occupational psychology background or with greater than 10 years

Charts 7-1 Listening vs speaking by location

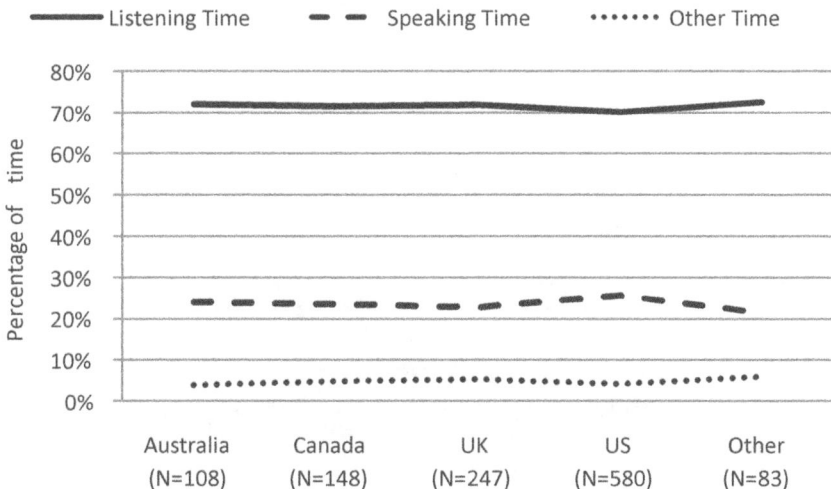

Legend: ——— Listening Time — — Speaking Time ••••••• Other Time

Y-axis: Percentage of time (0% to 80%)

X-axis:
Australia (N=108) Canada (N=148) UK (N=247) US (N=580) Other (N=83)

Chart 7-2 Listening vs speaking by background

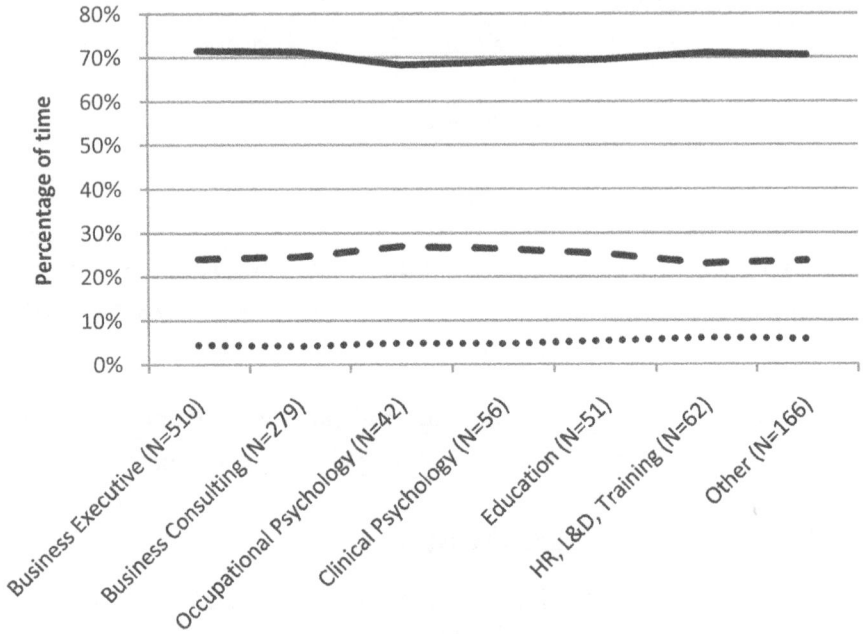

Chart 7-3 Listening vs speaking by experience

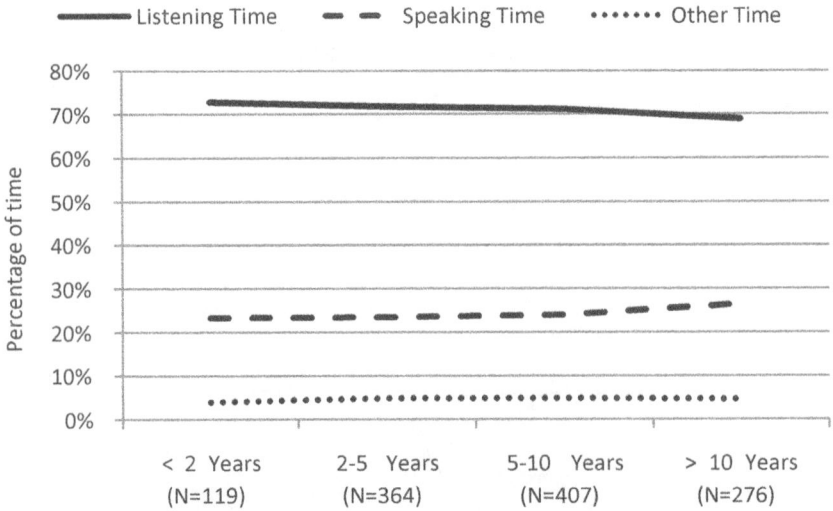

experience spend more time speaking and less time listening than their respective peers.

Across all three sets of groups, statistical tests show the data is not normalised and variables have heterogeneous variances. Therefore non-parametric Kruskal-Wallis with follow up Mann-Whitney tests are used.

The table below (7-4) shows that the mean ranking for the amount of time an executive coach is listening is statistically significantly affected by their experience; and the amount of time speaking is statistically significantly affected by their location and experience.   It also shows that any differences in background were not statistically significant (p>0.05) and are shown in grey italics.

Follow up analysis using Mann-Whitney show that executive coaches who live in the US (mean ranking: MR=434.1, mean: M=25.64, standard deviation: SD=8.832) speak more than coaches who live in the UK (MR=366.81, M=22.85, SD=8.350). The Mann-Whitney test is significant beyond the 0.01 level: U=59974.0; Monte Carlo p<0.005 (based on 10,000 sampled tables).

Table 7-4 Kruskal-Wallis tests for listening vs speaking

Statistical significant difference in mean rankings	Location	Background	Experience
Listening Time	*p>0.05*	*p>0.05*	$\chi^2 (3) = 17.199$ p<0.0005
Speaking Time	$\chi^2 (4) = 29.216$ p<0.0005	*p>0.05*	$\chi^2 (3) = 18.140$ p<0.0005
Other Time	*p>0.05*	*p>0.05*	*p>0.05*
Kruskal-Wallis test is significant beyond the 0.01 level Monte Carlo p based on 10,000 sampled tables *No statistically significant difference*			

Executive coaches with greater than 10 years experience (MR=317.92, M=68.91%, SD=10.400) listen less than coaches with 5-10 years experience (MR=358.33, M=71.17%, SD=10.582). The Mann-Whitney test is significant beyond the 0.01 level: U=49519.50; Monte Carlo p=0.01 (based on 10,000 sampled tables).

Executive coaches with greater than 10 years experience (MR=368.94, M=26.50%, SD=9.559) speak more than coaches with 5-10 years experience (MR=323.73, M=24.00%, SD=8.405). The Mann-Whitney test is significant beyond the 0.01 level: U=48731.00; Monte Carlo p=0.003 (based on 10,000 sampled tables).

In summary, executive coaches with the most experience have a tendency to speak more and listen less and those that live in the US have a tendency to speak more. However when comparing these results with the population means these results are not significant in the population for executive coaches living in the US, but are significant for those with most experience.

The Relevance of Linguistic Behaviours

The charts below and following pages (7-6, 7-7 and 7-8) show that executive coaches living in the US, from a clinical psychology background and those having more than 10 years experience (all shown in solid black) give higher average ratings to the more directive linguistic behaviours of *being a role model, providing ideas, explaining, offering guidance, instructing, giving advice* and *telling*.

Chart 7-6 Relevance of linguistic behaviours by location

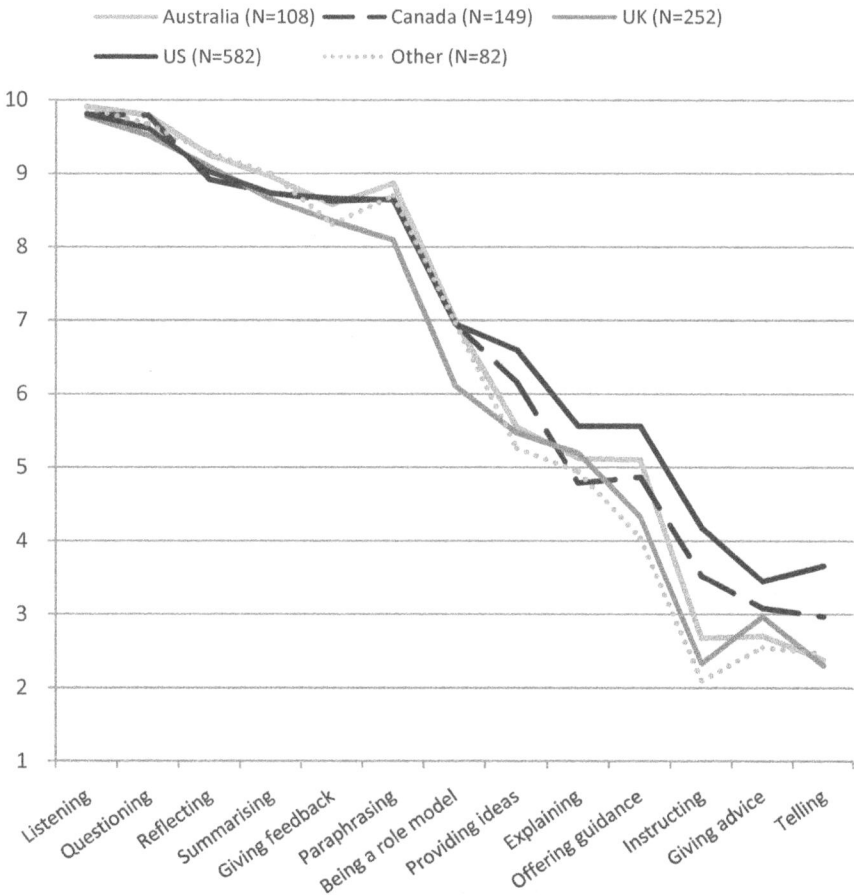

Chart 7-7 Relevance of Linguistic Behaviours by Background

- – • Business Executive (N=513)
- – – Business Consulting (N=280)
——— Occupational Psychology (N=43)
——— Clinical Psychology (N=57)
········ Education (N=52)
～～～ HR, L&D, Training (N=62)
～～～ Other (N=166)

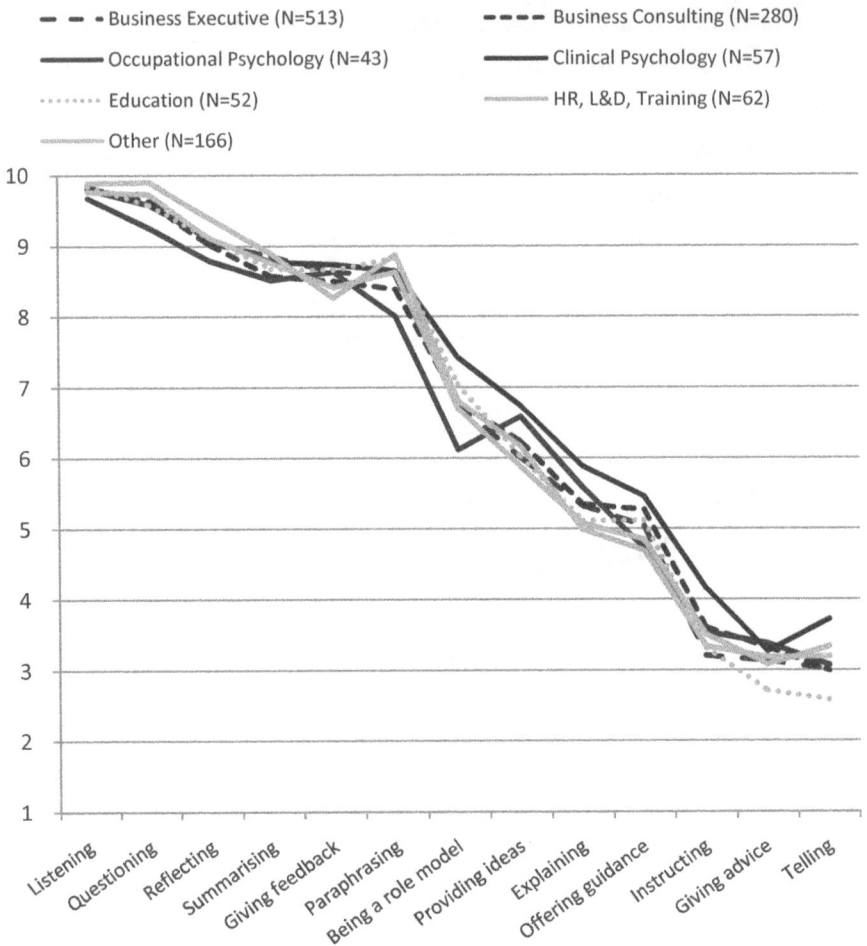

In addition executive coaches with more than 10 years experience give lower average ratings to the most non-directional of linguistic behaviours of *listening, questioning, reflecting* and *summarising*.

Chart 7-8 Relevance of Linguistic Behaviours by Experience

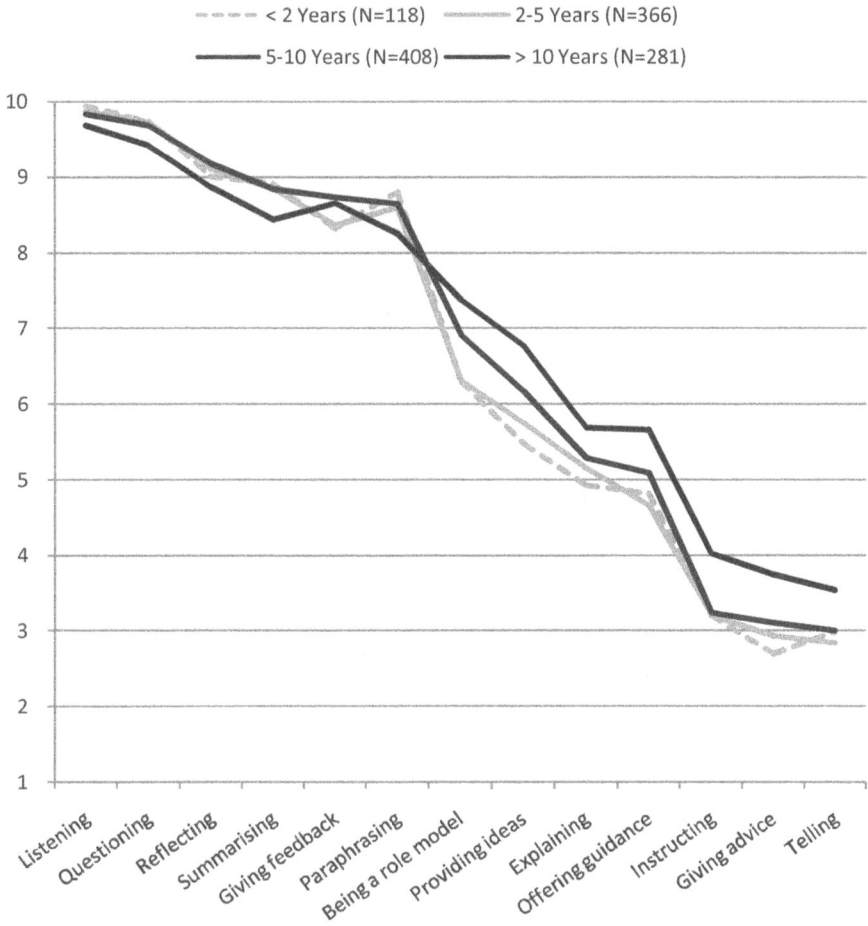

Across all three sets of groups, statistical tests show the data is not normalised and variables have heterogeneous variances. Therefore non-parametric Kruskal-Wallis with follow up Mann-Whitney tests are used.

The table below (7-9) confirms that the differences seen in the earlier charts for *location* (7-6) and *experience* (7-8) are statistically significant but does not confirm the differences seen in the chart for *background* (Figure 7-7) except for the relevance of *questioning*.

Table 7-9 Kruskal-Wallis tests for relevance of linguistic behaviours

Statistical significant difference in mean rankings	Location	Background	Experience
Listening	$p>0.05$	$p>0.05$	$X^2 (3)=10.774,$ $p=0.013$
Questioning	$p>0.05$	$X^2 (6) = 19.104$ $p=0.003$	$X^2 (3)=8.289,$ $p=0.040$
Reflecting	$p>0.05$	$p>0.05$	$p>0.05$
Summarising	$p>0.05$	$p>0.05$	$p>0.05$
Paraphrasing	$p>0.05$	$p>0.05$	$p>0.05$
Giving feedback	$p>0.05$	$p>0.05$	$p>0.05$
Being a role model	$X^2 (4)=19.913,$ $p<0.0005$	$p>0.05$	$X^2 (3)=28.487$ $p<0.0005$
Providing ideas	$X^2 (4)=52.84,$ $p<0.0005$	$p>0.05$	$X^2 (3)=34.265$ $p<0.0005$
Explaining	$X^2 (4)=16.725,$ $p=0.002$	$p>0.05$	$X^2 (3)=10.905,$ $p=0.014$
Offering guidance	$X^2 (4)=56.995,$ $p<0.0005$	$p>0.05$	$X^2 (3)=23.842$ $p<0.0005$
Instructing	$X^2 (4)=180.66,$ $p<0.0005$	$p>0.05$	$X^2 (3)=20.869$ $p<0.0005$
Giving advice	$X^2 (4)=22.387,$ $p<0.0005$	$p>0.05$	$X^2 (3)=23.283$ $p<0.0005$
Telling	$X^2 (4)=98.631$ $p<0.0005$	$p>0.05$	$X^2 (3)=15.218,$ $p=0.001$

Kruskal-Wallis test is significant beyond the 0.01 level
Monte Carlo p based on 10,000 sampled tables
No statistically significant difference

The table below (7-10) shows that executive coaches living in the US rate the relevance of certain linguistic behaviours higher (or lower in the case of *being a role model*) than the ratings from certain other countries. More specifically executive coaches living in the US rate the relevance of *telling* and *instructing* in executive coaching statistically significantly higher than

Table 7-10 Mann-Whitney tests for the relevance by location

Statistically significant differences by location	US v UK	US v Canada	US v Australia	US v Other
Being a role model	MR=3656 v 440.0 **M= 6.11 v 6.9 5** SD=2.638 v 2.753 U=60255.5 p<0.0005 Note: UK is higher!	*p>0.0125*	*p>0.0125*	*p>0.0125*
Providing ideas	MR=450.2 v 341.9 M=6.59 v 5.47 SD=2.505 v 2.407 U=54276 P<0.0005	*p>0.0125*	M=358.2v 277.2 M=6.59 v 5.55 SD=2.505 v 2.526 U=24046.5 P<0.0005	MR=344.6 v 246.9 **M=6.59 v 5.26** SD=2.505 v 2.619 U=16840 p<0.0005
Explaining	*p>0.0125*	MR=379.7 v 312.6 **M=5.56 v 4.79** SD=2.210 v 2.412 U=35400.5 p<0.0005	*p>0.0125*	*p>0.0125*
Offering guidance	MR=452.4 v 336.9 M=5.56 v 4.33 SD=2.547 v 2.381 U=53011 p<0.0005	MR=377.6 v 320.6 M=5.56 v 4.87 SD=2.547 v 2.622 U=36587 p=0.003	*p>0.0125*	MR=346.6 v 232.2 **M=5.56 v 4.04** SD=2.547 v 2.338 U=15637 p<0.0005
Instructing	MR=479.0 v 275.5 M=4.17 v 2.33 SD=2.357 v 1.707 U=37558.5 p<0.0005	MR=378.6 v 317.0 M=4.17 v 3.52 SD=2.357 v 2.262 U=36056.5 p=0.002	MR=367.2 v 228.6 M=4.17 v 2.68, SD=2.357 v 2.126 U=18797 p<0.0005	MR=354.9 v 173.7 **M=4.17 v 2.10** SD=2.357 v 1.375 U=10840.5 p<0.0005
Giving advice	MR=432.7 v 382.4 M=3.45v 2.97 SD=2.262 v 2.061 U=64492 p=0.004	*p>0.0125*	MR=356.0 v 289.0 M=3.45 v 2.70 SD=2.262 v 1.925 U=25326 p=0.001	MR=341.6 v 267.6 **M=3.45 v 2.55** SD=2.262 v 1.694 U=18542.5 p=0.001
Telling	MR=463.9 v 310.4 **M=3.66 v 2.30** SD=2.332 v 1.755 U=46329 p<0.0005	MR=379.2 v 317.0 M=3.66 v 2.97 SD=2.332 v 2.032 U=36688 p=0.001	MR=364.1 v 245.1 M=3.66 v 2.38 SD=2.332 v 1.786 U=20589.5 p<0.0005	MR=345.1 v 243.4 M=3.66 v 2.46 SD=2.332 v 1.687 U=16555.5 p<0.0005
Mann-Whitney test (U) significant beyond the 0.01 level Monte Carlo p based on 10,000 sampled tables *No statistically significant difference, Monte Carlo p>0.0125 with Bonferroni correction* MR = mean ranking, M = mean of rating for each behaviour, SD = standard deviation				

all other countries; *giving advice* and *providing ideas* higher than all other countries except Canada; *offering guidance* higher than all other countries except Australia; and *explaining* higher than Canada.

Comparison with the population means shows that the differences may also be considered statistically significant in the population.

The table below (7-11) shows that executive coaches with an *occupational psychology* background rate the relevance of *questioning* statistically significantly lower than coaches from a *business consulting* background. Comparison with the population means show that these differences may also be considered significant in the population.

Table 7-11 Mann-Whitney tests for the relevance by background

Statistical significant differences by background	Occupational psychology vs Business consulting	Occupational psychology	Business consulting
Questioning	MR=131.6 v 166.7 U=4712.5, p=0.002	M=9.26 SD=1.115	M=9.62 SD=1.047
Mann-Whitney test significant beyond the 0.01 level Monte Carlo p based on 10,000 sampled tables *No statistically significant difference, Monte Carlo p>0.05 with Bonferroni correction* MR = mean ranking, M = mean of rating for each behaviour, SD = standard deviation			

The table opposite (7-12) shows that executive coaches with *greater than 10 years experience* rate the relevance of certain linguistic behaviours higher or lower than coaches with *5-10 years of experience*. More specifically those with most experience rate the relevance of *telling, giving advice, instructing, offering guidance, explaining, providing ideas* and *being a role model* statistically significantly higher; and *questioning* and *listening* statistically significantly lower.

Table 7-12 Mann-Whitney tests for the relevance by experience

Statistical significant differences by experience	>10 years experience vs 5-10 years experience	>10 Years experience	5-10 Years experience
'>10 years experience' lower for:			
Listening	MR=334.88 v 351.97 U=54479, p=0.050	M=9.69 SD=1.106	M=9.83 SD=0.676
Questioning	MR=330.54 v 354.96 U=53261.5, p=0.028	M=9.42 SD=1.44	M=9.68 SD=0.859
'>10 years experience' higher for:			
Being a role model	MR=367 v 329.85 U=51143, p=0.016	M=7.38 SD=2.541	M=6.92 SD=2.611
Providing ideas	MR=373.33 v 325.49 U=49362, p=0.002	M=6.76 SD=2.476	M=6.16 SD=2.551
Explaining	MR=365.03 v 331.2 U=51695, p=0.025	M=5.68 SD=2.456	M=5.28 SD=2.204
Offering guidance	MR=370.22 v 327.63 U=50237, p=0.004	M=5.65 SD=2.621	M=5.08 SD=2.594
Instructing	MR=379.06 v 321.54 U=47752.5, p<0.0005	M=4.02 SD=2.547	M=3.24 SD=2.146
Giving advice	MR=374.42 v 324.74 U=49058, p=0.00	M=3.74 SD=2.469	M=3.11 SD=2.12
Telling	MR=368.43 v 328.86 U=50739, p=0.008	M=3.53 SD=2.401	M=3.00 SD=2.064

Mann-Whitney test significant beyond the 0.01 level
Monte Carlo p based on 10,000 sampled tables
No statistically significant difference, Monte Carlo p>0.05 with Bonferroni correction
MR = mean ranking, M = mean of rating for each behaviour, SD = standard deviation

Comparison with the population means show that these differences between executive coaches with greater than 10 years experience and those with 5-10 years experience may be considered statistically significant in the population for *listening, questioning, instructing, giving advice* and *telling*.

The Use of Speaking Behaviours

The charts below and on the following pages (7-14, 7-15 and 7-16) show that on average coaches from all countries, all backgrounds and all experience place the speaking behaviours in the same order. The charts show that executive coaches who live in the US rank their use of *telling and instructing* and *providing ideas and guidance* higher compared with all other countries. Those from a clinical psychology background rank their

Chart 7-14 The use of speaking behaviours by country

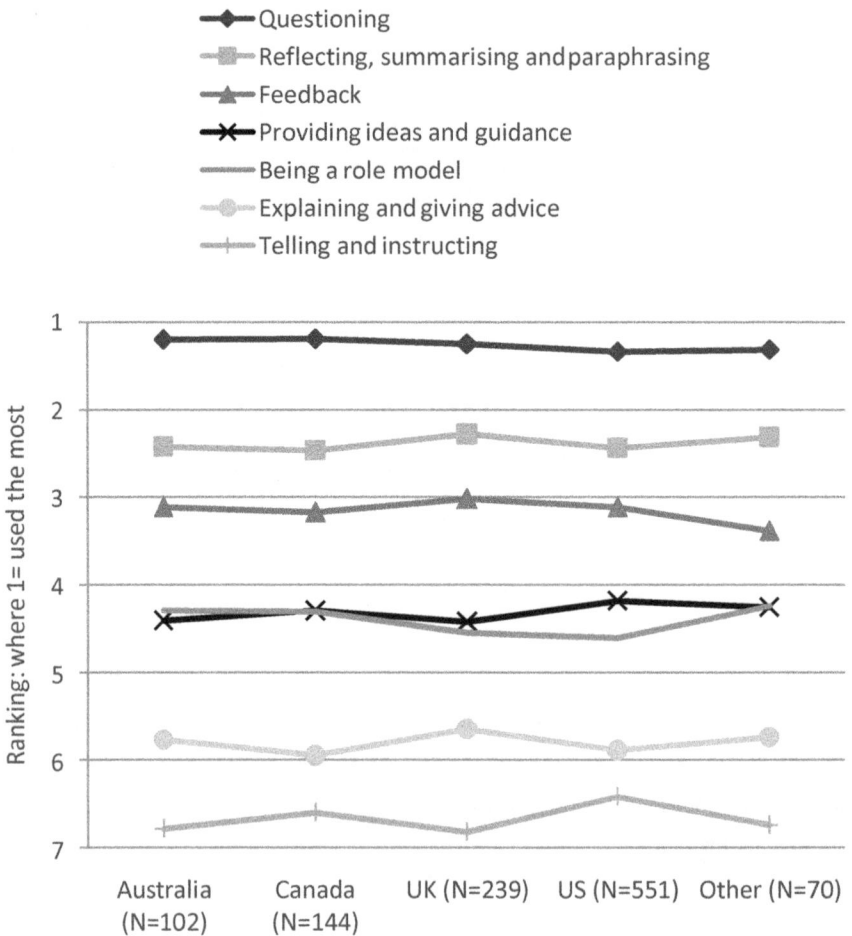

Legend:
- Questioning
- Reflecting, summarising and paraphrasing
- Feedback
- Providing ideas and guidance
- Being a role model
- Explaining and giving advice
- Telling and instructing

Y-axis: Ranking: where 1= used the most

X-axis: Australia (N=102), Canada (N=144), UK (N=239), US (N=551), Other (N=70)

use of *questioning* and *reflecting, summarising and paraphrasing* lower when compared with other backgrounds and also rank their use of *being a role model* higher. Those with most experience rank their use of *questioning* and *reflecting, summarising and paraphrasing* lower and rank their use of *telling and instructing* and *explaining and giving advice* higher than those with less experience.

Chart 7-15 The use of speaking behaviours by background

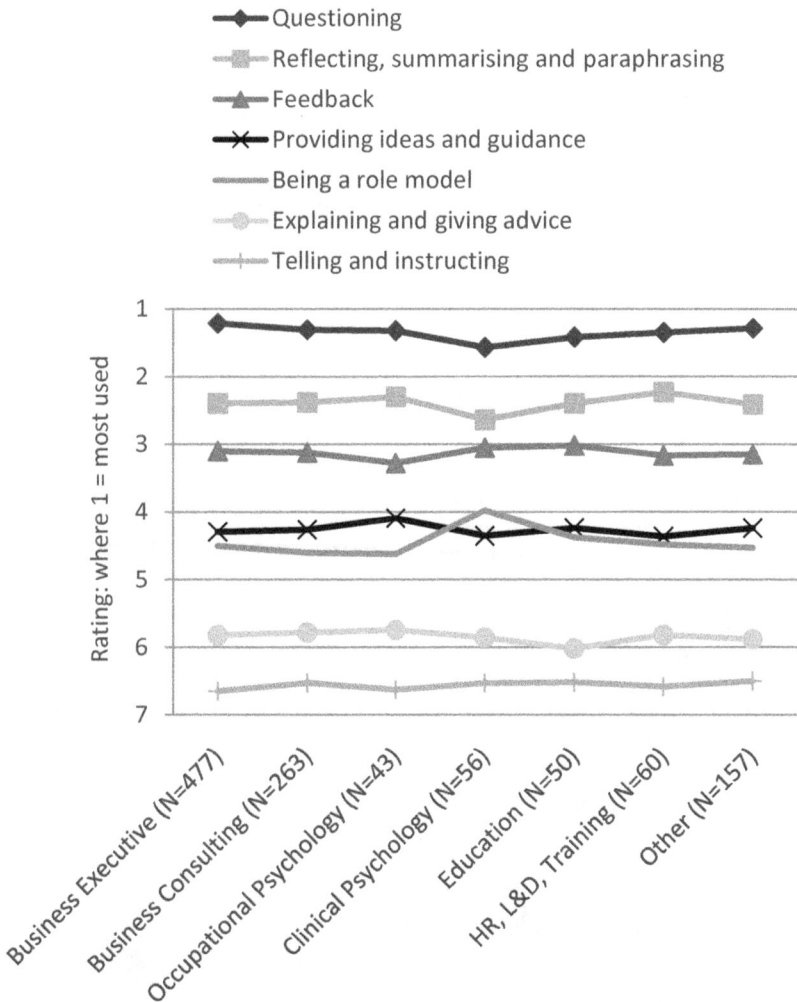

Non-parametric tests are used for the analysis as the scale of this question is ordinal: based on the ranking in order of use. Note that for the purpose of creating a visual summary and representation of the groups, average rankings are used. The statistical analysis used Kruskal-Wallis and Mann-Whitney tests.

Chart 7-16 The use of speaking behaviours by experience

- Questioning
- Reflecting, summarising and paraphrasing
- Feedback
- Providing ideas and guidance
- Being a role model
- Explaining and giving advice
- Telling and instructing

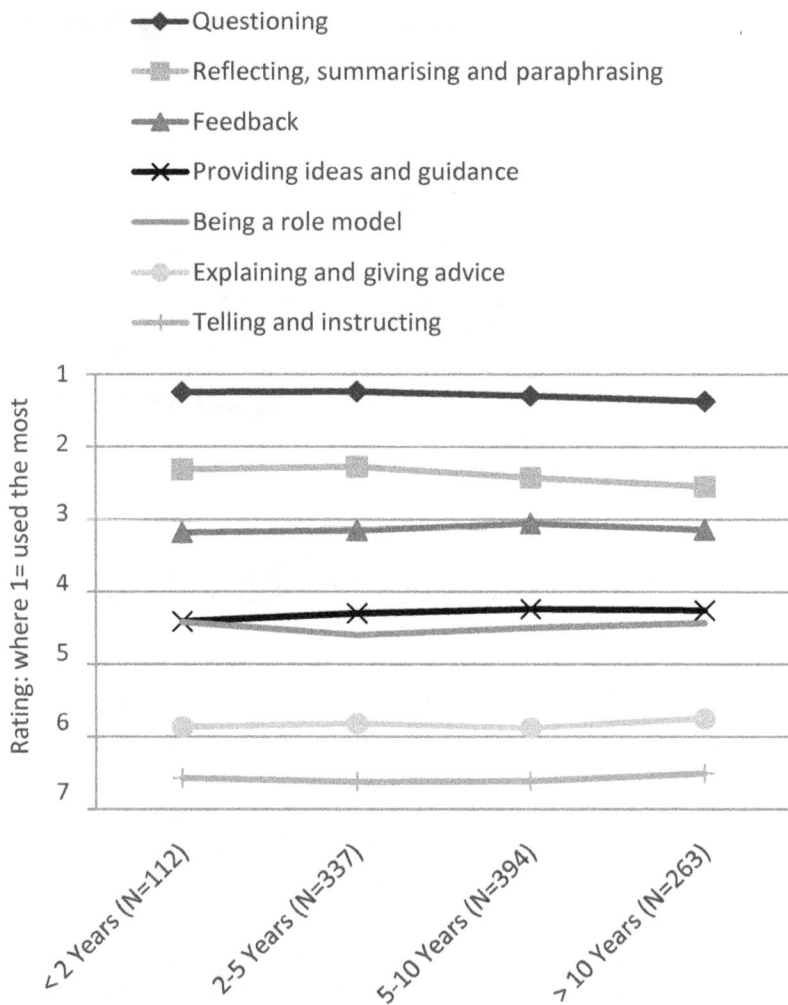

The table below (7-17) shows four of the speaking behaviours by *location* and *questioning* by *background* have statistically significant differences.

Table 7-17 Kruskal-Wallis tests for use of speaking behaviours

Statistical significant difference in mean rankings	Location	Background	Experience
Questioning	x^2 (4) =11.231, p=0.025	x^2 (6) =18.480, p =0.003	*p>0.05*
Reflecting, Summarising & Paraphrasing	*p>0.05*	*p>0.05*	*p>0.05*
Feedback	*p>0.05*	*p>0.05*	*p>0.05*
Being a role model	*p>0.05*	*p>0.05*	*p>0.05*
Providing ideas and guidance	x^2 (4) =10.252, p=0.038	*p>0.05*	*p>0.05*
Explaining and giving advice	x^2 (4) =23.301, p<0.0005	*p>0.05*	*p>0.05*
Telling and instructing	x^2 (4) =77.176, p<0.0005	*p>0.05*	*p>0.05*
Kruskal-Wallis test is significant beyond the 0.01 level Monte Carlo p based on 10,000 sampled tables *No statistically significant difference*			

Further analysis in the table on the next page (7-18) reveals that executive coaches living in the US rank their use of *telling and instructing* statistically significantly higher than all other countries. They rank their use of *providing ideas and guidance* higher and *explaining and giving advice* lower than coaches living in the UK.

Executive coaches with a background in clinical psychology rank their use of *questioning* (MR=316.07) statistically significantly lower than those with a business executive background (MR=261.24). The Mann-Whitney test is significant beyond the 0.01 level: U=10608; Monte Carlo p<0.0005 (based on 10,000 sampled tables).

Table 7-18 Mann-Whitney tests for use of speaking behaviours by location

Statistically significant differences by location	US v UK	US v Canada	US v Australia	US v Other
Questioning	*p>0.0125*	MR=355.9 v 317.6 U=35295.5 p=0.006	*p>0.0125*	*p>0.0125*
Providing ideas and guidance	MR=381.1 v 428.8 U=57884 p=0.003	*p>0.0125*	*p>0.0125*	*p>0.0125*
Explaining and giving advice	MR=416.3 v 347.5 U=54389 p<0.0005	*p>0.0125*	*p>0.0125*	*p>0.0125*
Telling and instructing	MR=362.0 v 472.8 U=47371 p<0.0005	MR=339.3 v 381.3 U=34875 p=0.010	MR=396 v 314.2 U=21064 p<0.0005	MR=303.3 v 372 U=15015 p<0.0005
Mann-Whitney test (U) significant beyond the 0.01 level Monte Carlo p based on 10,000 sampled tables *No statistically significant difference* *Monte Carlo p>0.0125 with Bonferroni correction* MR = mean ranking				

Summary

The demographic analysis is based on the grouping of:

- where executive coaches live (location)

- their business background

- how long they have been practicing executive coaching (experience)

Overall the analysis shows almost universal agreement in the relative relevance and use of each linguistic behaviour. There is general agreement, regardless of location, background or experience, that *listening* and *questioning* are most relevant and used, and that *telling*, *giving advice* and *instructing* are least relevant and used.

However there are some statistically significant differences between the groups:

1. Executive coaches with the most experience speak more and listen less; they think *listening* and *questioning* are less relevant while *instructing, giving advice* and *telling* are more relevant.

2. Executive coaching living in the US think *telling* and *instructing* are more relevant and use them more and think *giving advice, providing ideas and offering guidance* are more relevant.

3. Executive coaches with *occupational psychology* backgrounds think *questioning* is less relevant.

4. Executive coaches with *clinical psychology* backgrounds use *questioning* less.

Chapter 8

The Linguistic Landscape™

This chapter will take the results and analysis presented in the previous chapter and draw out the major conclusions and formally answer the research questions and hypotheses:

Hypothesis 3, that a coach spends more time listening than speaking in the practice of executive coaching in the English language, is proven and over 98% of coaches spend more time listening than speaking in the practice of executive coaching in the English language and most spend considerably more time listening.

Hypothesis 4, that the non-directive linguistic behaviours of listening, questioning, reflecting, summarising and paraphrasing are the most relevant and used in the practice of executive coaching in the English language, is proven and the non-directive linguistic behaviours of *listening, questioning, reflecting, summarising* and *paraphrasing* are the most relevant and used in the practice of executive coaching in the English language. However there is also a clear distinction that places *listening* and *questioning* as the key linguistic behaviours for an executive coach.

Hypothesis 5, that the linguistic behaviours of being a role model and feedback are relevant and used in the practice of executive coaching in the English language, is not proven, as it has been shown that *being a role model* is not a linguistic behaviour and the linguistic behaviour of *giving feedback* should be considered to be one of the behaviours most relevant and used in the practice of executive coaching in the English language.

Hypothesis 6, that the directive linguistic behaviours of telling, instructing, giving advice, providing ideas, offering guidance and explaining are not relevant or used in the practice of executive coaching in the English language, is partially proven as it has been shown that the linguistic behaviours of *telling, instructing* and *giving advice* are not relevant or used in the practice of executive coaching in the English language. However is has also been shown that the linguistic behaviours of *providing ideas, offering guidance* and *explaining* may be relevant and used by many executive coaches in certain circumstances.

These hypotheses illustrate that there is a clear hierarchy in the relevance and use of different linguistic behaviours, but that there are some disagreements regarding the relevance and use of the most directive behaviours.

Hypothesis 7 is that the relevance and use of directive linguistic behaviours of telling, instructing, giving advice, providing ideas, offering guidance and explaining are determined by the location (7a), background (7b) and experience (7c) of an executive coach.

Hypothesis 7a is partially proven as coaches who live in the US think that the directive linguistic behaviours of *telling, instructing, giving advice, providing ideas, offering guidance* and *explaining* are more relevant and use *telling* and *instructing* more.

Hypothesis 7b is not proven. However it was proved that the relevance and use of questioning is impacted by background, although in a fairly limited way.

Hypothesis 7c is partially proven and coaches with the most experience think that the directive linguistic behaviours of *telling, instructing* and *giving advice* are more relevant. They also think that *questioning* and *listening* are less relevant and use them less.

The final conclusion is that on average there is global universal agreement on the hierarchy of the relevance and use of linguistic behaviours in the practice of executive coaching in the English language, regardless of location, background or experience. However there are some executive coaches who have very different views on the relevance and use of linguistic behaviours that were at odds with the vast majority.

It might be concluded that what they are delivering is more akin to consulting or mentoring. As was discovered in the literature review there are some who do not delineate between coaches and consultants.

Alternatively it has been suggested that those with the most experience, by mastering the art of executive coaching find an effective way to use directional activities in their practice. Or could it be that the industry has changed and left behind its roots of directional activity? Ives asserts this but also suggests that the industry is again becoming more directional. (Ives, 2008) However this research has found no evidence to support that theory. The answer to his question "may a coach also tell?" is "Yes but only when s/he stops coaching."

What are the most relevant and used linguistic behaviours for an executive coach? The simplest answer is *listening* and *questioning*. This research confirms they are indeed the core behaviours. Goldberg suggests that coaching is 85% questioning. (Goldberg, 1999) And this research proves that linguistically executive coaching is 70% listening and that the rest is predominantly questioning.

The literature review highlighted one coaching model that listed linguistic behaviours and that proposed an order based on how directive these behaviours were. (Downey, 2003) It turns out that executive coaches generally rate the relevance and rank the usage of the non-directive behaviours as the most relevant and used.

Questioning is perhaps the most marked difference as it gains universal support that places it neck-and-neck with listening as the most important linguistic behaviour. However there are many additions suggested from both the literature review and this research. As a result there have been a number of changes: *providing ideas*, *listening* and *questioning* were re-defined and five new categories created: *acknowledging, explaining, sharing stories, silence* and *telling*.

The new concepts of *acknowledging* can be grouped with *feedback,* and *sharing stories* with *providing ideas* as they are closely aligned in the qualitative analysis. There is at this time no evidence to group *Silence* reliably. However *silence* surrounds all linguistic behaviour, without it there would be no words, only noise! So until more research has clarified its position, it gains a special place encompassing the Landscape..

This global survey of 1,190 qualified executive coaches provided quantitative data and over 6,000 words of feedback, that make it possible to be sure which linguistic behaviours are most relevant; that in turn can inform how coaches are trained, how they conduct their practice and where future researchers may focus their attention. Before moving on to those recommendations, it only remains to present a new model of behaviour called **The Linguistic Landscape™ of Executive Coaching** (shown opposite, 8-1) and to recommend this to practitioners, academics and teachers of executive coaching.

Figure 8-1 The Linguistic Landscape™ of Executive Coaching

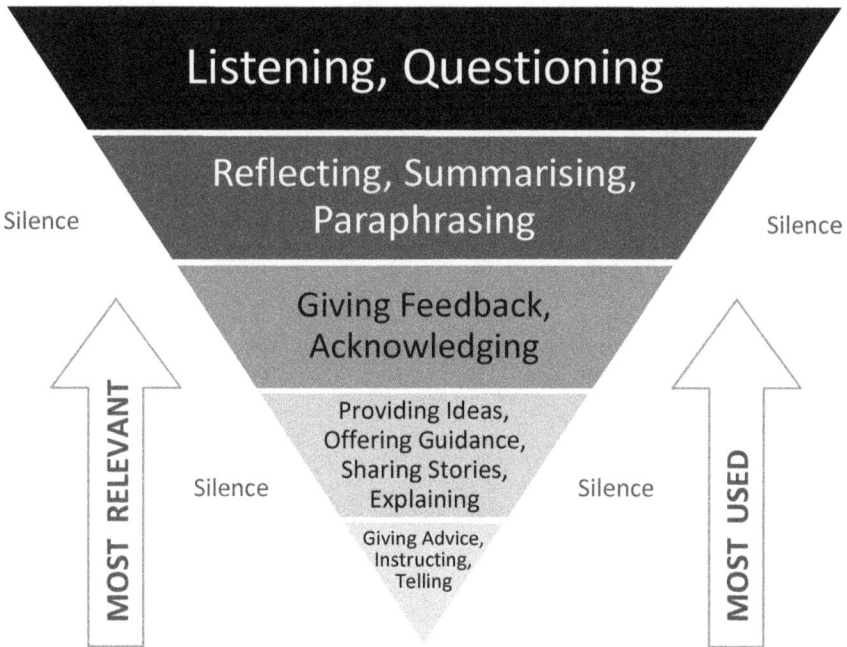

© William Pennington 2009

Chapter 9

Recommendations

This chapter makes recommendations for future academic research followed by suggestions for practitioners, training organisations and professional bodies.

Future Academic Research

The Definition and Delineation of Executive Coaching

This research has proposed a new definition for executive coaching and it is recommended that the next step will be to test and develop this further. This can be done with a broader audience that includes all three elements of the triad i.e. executive coaches, executives and sponsors in organisations and in multiple languages on a global scale.

Qualitative research, possibly in the form of focus groups, surveys and interviews would enable the concepts and descriptions to be refined and modified further, while another quantitative survey would be needed to ensure the definition is considered universally accepted. If time and resources allow this researcher would highly recommend a mixed methods approach combining the best that qualitative and quantitative methods can offer.

It is recommended that a similar process of research is undertaken into the definitions and delineation of the various other relevant niches of coaching, including life, business, personal and team.

It is also recommended that a valuable opportunity exists to investigate the forms of coaching that are purchased by organisations and how the triadic relationship is managed in each case.

The Linguistic Landscape™ of Executive Coaching:

This research proposes a new Linguistic Landscape™ of Executive Coaching and it is recommended that the following research questions are answered in order to develop it further:

- What is the quantitative relevance and use of silence, acknowledgement and sharing stories in the practice of executive coaching?

- What changes to the linguistic landscape would result from incorporating the views of executives and observing coaching sessions?

- What changes to the linguistic landscape would make a model applicable for all coaching?

The final recommendation is that within the linguistic landscape the following research questions are answered:

- The tools and models of questioning - how can they be used effectively in coaching?

- Which linguistic behaviours are the most useful for delivering feedback of 360 degree and self-assessment reports in executive coaching?

- What is the impact that non-verbal linguistic behaviours (e.g. laughing and natural exclamations) have in coaching?

Practitioners, Trainers and Professional Bodies

The definition and delineation of the coaching profession is the most important challenge for the industry. It is recommended that the proposed definition for executive coaching be taken and developed alongside similar projects for each of the major niches of coaching.

The research highlighted a need for additional clarity around the ethics of the triadic relationship in executive coaching. It is recommended that there are much clearer ethical statements that state if an organisation pays for coaching then they are the sponsor and need to be taken into account in the contracting and delivery.

Giving Feedback in executive coaching is a particularly important linguistic behaviour. It is proposed that the feedback model presented in this research is used as an architecture to develop executive coaching skills. The feedback model differentiated between three types of feedback: from the organisation, a client's self assessment and the coach. It is suggested that together with the Linguistic Landscape™, these provide executive coaches with useful tools to enable more effective feedback of 360 degree self-assessment reports. They also provide a powerful framework in which to provide feedback from a coach's own observations and intuitions in a coaching session.

Questioning is a key behaviour and skill that has not been given enough attention in the coaching world. It is recommended that practitioners and training organisations focus more on questioning. There are many questioning models that could be mapped into the coaching context and made available for practitioners.

Chapter 10

References

Adams, M. (2008). *Top 12 Reasons to Ask Questions*. Retrieved 24th July 2008, from http://qstorming.com/

Altman, W. (2007). Executive Coaching Comes of Age. *Engineering Management Journal, 17,* 26-29.

Alvey, S. & Barclay, K. (2007). The characteristics of dyadic trust in executive coaching (Vol. 1, pp. 18-27).

Anderson, S. (2005). Career / Life Coaching. In H. Morgan, P. Harkins & M. Goldsmith (Eds.), *The Art and Practice of Leadership Coaching* (pp. 110-112). New Jersey: Wiley.

Angus, M. (2008). Managing and leading people. *Training Journal,* 56.

Baker, M. (2005). Career / Life Coaching. In H. Morgan, P. Harkins & M. Goldsmith (Eds.), *The Art and Practice of Leadership Coaching* (pp. 117-120). New Jersey: Wiley.

Bandler, R. & Grinder, J. (1975). *The Structure of Magic.* Palo Alto, CA: Science and Behavior Books.

Barnes, K. (2005). Coaching Leaders / Behavioral Coaching. In H. Morgan, P. Harkins & M. Goldsmith (Eds.), *The Art and Practice of Leadership Coaching* (pp. 85-86). New Jersey: Wiley.

Bartlett, C. A. (2005). Coaching the Top Team. In H. Morgan, P. Harkins & M. Goldsmith (Eds.), *The Art and Practice of Leadership Coaching* (pp. 199-202). New Jersey: Wiley.

Bluckert, P. (2005). Critical factors in executive coaching - the coaching relationship. *Industrial and Commercial Training, 37*(7), 336-340.

Bolt, J. (2005). Coaching for Leadership Development. In H. Morgan, P. Harkins & M. Goldsmith (Eds.), *The Art and Practice of Leadership Coaching* (pp. 143-145). New Jersey: Wiley.

Bresser, F. & Wilson, C. (2006). What is coaching? In J. Passmore (Ed.), *Excellence in Coaching: The Industry Guide*. London: Kogan Press.

Carey, T. A. & Mullan, R. J. (2004). What Is Socratic Questioning? *Psychotherapy, 41*(3), 217-226.

Carey, T. A. & Mullan, R. J. (2007). Socratic questioning in psychotherapy: A history of crossed purposes. *Counselling Psychology Review- British Psychological Society, 22*, 20-30.

Carter, A. (2001). The trainer as executive coach How does executive coaching work from a coach's perspective? What makes a good executive coach? And how can trainers develop their skills in this area? *Training Journal*, 13-15.

Charvet, S. R. (1997). *Words that change minds : mastering the language of influence* (2nd ed.). Dubuque, Iowa: Kendall/Hunt Pub. Co.

Clarke, J. & Dembkowski, D. S. (2006). The Art of Asking Great Questions. *The International Journal of Mentoring and Coaching, IV*(2).

Clutterbuck, D. & Lane, G. (2004). *The situational mentor : an international review of competences and capabilities in mentoring*. Aldershot: Gower.

The Concise Oxford Dictionary of English Etymology. (1996). Retrieved 8th April 2008, from http://www.oxfordreference.com/

Corbett, K. (2008). *Sherpa Executive Coaching Survey 2008*. Retrieved 20th August 2008, from http://www.sherpacoaching.com/

Corbett, K. (2009). *Sherpa Executive Coaching Survey 2009*. Retrieved 6th February 2009, from http://www.sherpacoaching.com/

Creswell, J. W. (2003). *Research design : qualitative, quantitative, and mixed methods approaches* (2nd ed. ed.). Thousand Oaks, Calif. ; London: Sage.

Creswell, J. W. (2009). *Research design : qualitative, quantitative, and mixed methods approaches* (3rd ed. ed.). Los Angeles ; London: Sage.

Dilts, R. (1999). *Sleight of mouth : the magic of conversational belief change*. Capitola, Calif.: Meta Publications.

Dilts, R. & DeLozier, J. (2000). *Encyclopedia of systemic neuro-linguistic programming and NLP new coding*. Scotts Valley, Calif.: NLP University Press.

Dove, J. (2004). NLP and coaching. *Selection and Development Review, 20*(4), 6-8.

Downey, M. (2003). *Effective coaching*: New York; London: Texere, 2001 (2002 [printing]).

Dunbar, A. (2005). Using Metaphors with Coaching, *The Bulletin for the Assocation of Coaching* (Vol. 6, pp. 2-4). London.

Elkington, J. (2009). Stirring of a New Order. *Director, 62*(8), 24.

Feldman, D. C. & Lankau, M. J. (2005). Executive Coaching: A Review and Agenda for Future Research. *Journal of Management, 31*(6), 829-848.

Field, A. (2005). *Discovering statistics using SPSS : (and sex, drugs and rock'n'roll)* (2nd ed.). London: Sage.

Gale, J., Liljenstrand, A., Pardieu, J. & Nebeker, D. M. (2002). *Coaching: Who, what, where, when and how. Executive Summary of Coaching Practices*. Retrieved 22nd September 2008, from http://www.coachfederation.org/

Goldberg-Adams, M., Schiller, M & Cooperrider, D. L. (2004). With our questions we make the world. *Advances in Appreciative Inquiry, 1*, 105-124.

Goldberg, M. C. (1998). *The art of the question : a guide to short-term question-centered therapy*. New York; Chichester: Wiley.

Goldberg, M. C. (1999). Expert Question Asking: The Engine of Successful Coaching. *The Manchester Review*.

Goldsmith, M. (2002). *Coaching and Feedback*. Retrieved 15th August 2008, from http://www.marshallgoldsmithlibrary.com/

Goodwin, S. F. (2007). *RBS Corporate Responsibility Report*. Retrieved 22nd April 2009, from http://www.rbs.com/

Gordon, S. (2008). Appreciative inquiry coaching. *International Coaching Psychology Review, 3*, 19-31.

Grant, A. M. & Cavanagh, M. J. (2004). Toward a profession of coaching: Sixty-five years of progress and challenges for the future. *International Journal of Evidence Based Coaching and Mentoring 2*(1).

Gray, D. E. (2006). Executive Coaching: Towards a Dynamic Alliance of Psychotherapy and Transformative Learning Processes. *Management Learning, 37*, 475-498.

Gregory, J. B., Levy, P. E. & Jeffers, M. (2008). Development of a model of the feedback process within executive coaching. *Consulting Psychology Journal: Practice & Research, 60*(1), 42-56.

Hair, J. F. (2003). *Essentials of business research methods*. Hoboken, N.J.: Wiley.

Hall, D. T., Otazo, K. L. & Hollenbeck, G. P. (1999). Behind closed doors: What really happens in executive coaching. *Organizational Dynamics, 27*(3), 39-53.

Harland, P. (2006). Keeping it Clean. *The Model, 2*.

Hayes, P. (2006). *NLP coaching*. Maidenhead: Open University Press.

Hedman, A. (2001). The Person-Centred Approach. In B. Peltier (Ed.), *The psychology of executive coaching : theory and application* (pp. 66-80). New York ; Hove: Brunner-Routledge.

Helgesen, S. (2005). Coaching Anthropology. In H. Morgan, P. Harkins & M. Goldsmith (Eds.), *The Art and Practice of Leadership Coaching* (pp. 161-165). New Jersey: Wiley.

Hieker, C. & Huffington, C. (2006). Reflexive questions in a coaching psychology context. *International Coaching Psychology Review, 1*(2), 46-55.

ICF. (2007). *Global Coaching Survey*. Retrieved 20th August 2008, from http://www.coachfederation.org/

ICF. (2008). *ICF Code of Ethics*. Retrieved 16th April 2009, from http://www.coachfederation.org/

ITAA. (2009). *A summary of Transactional Analysis key ideas*. Retrieved 28th April 2009, from http://www.itaa-net.org/

Ives, Y. (2008). What is 'Coaching'? An Exploration of Conflicting Paradigms. *International Journal of Evidence Based Coaching and Mentoring 6*(2).

Jaworski, J. (1996). *Synchronicity: The Inner Path of Leadership*. San Francisco, CA: Berrett-Koehler.

Johnson, R. B. & Onwuegbuzie, A. J. (2004). Mixed Methods Research: A Research Paradigm Whose Time Has Come. *Educational Researcher, 33*(7), 14-26.

Joo, B. K. (2005). Executive Coaching: A Conceptual Framework From an Integrative Review of Practice and Research. *Human Resource Development Review, 4*, 462-488.

Kampa-Kokesch, S. & Anderson, M. Z. (2001). Executive Coaching: A Comprehensive Review of the Literature. *Consulting Psychology Journal, 53*(4), 205-228.

Kilburg, R. R. (1996). Towards a conceptual understanding and definition of executive coaching. *Consulting Psychology Journal: Practice & Research, 48*(2), 134-144.

Kouzes, J. (2005). Coaching for Credibility. In H. Morgan, P. Harkins & M. Goldsmith (Eds.), *The Art and Practice of Leadership Coaching* (pp. 61-66). New Jersey: Wiley.

Lawley, J. & Tomkins, P. (2004). Clean Language Revisited: The evolution of a model. *Rapport.*

Lawley, J. & Tomkins, P. (2006). Coaching with Metaphor. *Cutting Edge Coaching Techniques Handbook.*

Lawley, J. & Tompkins, P. (2000). *Metaphors in mind : transformation through symbolic modelling.* London: Developing Company Press.

Leedham, M. (2008). If Silence is Golden, does a coach talk too much?, *The Bulletin for the Assocation of Coaching* (Vol. 14, pp. 6-7). London.

Liljenstrand, A. M. (2004). *A comparison of practices and approaches to coaching based on academic background.* Unpublished Ph.D., Alliant International University, San Diego, United States -- California.

Linder-Pelz, S. & Hall, L. M. (2007). The theoretical roots of NLP-based coaching. *The Coaching Psychologist, 3*(1), 12-17.

Mador, M. (Ed.). (2006). *Research Methods.* Kingston: Kinston Business School.

Marquardt, M. J. (2005). *Leading with questions : how leaders find the right solutions by knowing what to ask* (1st ed. ed.). San Francisco, Calif.: Jossey-Bass ; Chichester : John Wiley [distributor].

McDermott, I. & Jago, W. (2001). *The NLP coach : a comprehensive guide to personal well-being & professional success*. London: Piatkus.

McElroy, M. (2009). *World's First True Sustainability Index (TM) announced*. Retrieved 23rd April 2009, from http://www.csrwire.com/

Mehrabian, A. (1981). *Silent messages: Implicit communication of emotions and attitudes*. Belmont, CA: Wadsworth.

Mehrabian, A. (2009). *Personality & Emotion Tests & Software; Psychological Books & Articles of Popular Interest* Retrieved 15th July 2009, fromhttp://www.kaaj.com/psych/smorder.html

Merriam-Webster. (2009). *Merriam-Webser Online Dictionary*. Retrieved 28th April 2009, from http://www.merriam-webster.com/

Morgan, H., Harkins, P. & Goldsmith, M. (2005). *The Art and Practice of Leadership Coaching*. New Jersey: Wiley.

Natale, S. M. & Diamante, T. (2005). The Five Stages of Executive Coaching: Better Process Makes Better Practice. *Journal of Business Ethics, 59*(4), 361-374.

O'Connor, J. S. & Lages, A. (2007). *How coaching works : the essential guide to the history and practice of effective coaching*. London: A. & C. Black.

Orem, S., Binkert, J. & Clancy, A. L. (2007). *Appreciative coaching : a positive process for change* (1st ed.). San Francisco, Calif.: Jossey-Bass ; Chichester : John Wiley [distributor].

Orenstein, R. L. (2002). Executive Coaching: It's Not Just About the Executive. *Journal of Applied Behavioral Science, 38*(3), 355-374.

Orenstein, R. L. (2006). Measuring Executive Coaching Efficacy? The Answer Was Right Here All the Time. *Consulting Psychology Journal, 58*(2), 106-116.

Owen, N. (2001). *The magic of metaphor : 77 stories for teachers, trainers & thinkers*: Carmarthen : Crown House.

The Oxford Dictionary of English (revised edition). (2005). Retrieved 20th August 2008, from http://www.oxfordreference.com/

Passmore, J. (2006). Introduction. In J. Passmore (Ed.), *Excellence in Coaching: The Industry Guide*. London: Kogan Press.

Passmore, J. & Gibbes, C. (2007). The state of executive coaching research: What does the current literature tell us and what's next for coaching research? *International Coaching Psychology Review, 2*(2), 116-128.

Rayner, G. (2009). The Downfall How one deal too many ruined RBS. *The Daily Telegraph,* p. 6.

Reeves, W. B. (2006). The Value Proposition for Executive Coaching. *Financial Executive, 22,* 48-50.

Sapir, E. (1929). The Status of Linguistics as a Science. In D. G. Mandelbaum (Ed.), *Culture, Language and Personality*. Berkeley, CA: University of California Press.

Saunders, M., Lewis, P. & Thornhill, A. (2006). *Research methods for business students* (4th ed.). Harlow: Financial Times Prentice Hall.

Sechrest, L. & Sidani, S. (1995). Quantitative and qualitative methods: Is There an Alternative? *Evaluation and Program Planning, 18*(1), 77-87.

Sherman, S. & Freas, A. (2004). The Wild West of Executive Coaching. *Harvard Business Review, 82*(11), 82-93.

Sieler, A. (2003). *Coaching to the Human Soul*. Victoria, Australia: Newfield, Australia.

Sparrow, S. (2007). Model behaviour. *Training & Coaching Today,* 24-25.

Sperry, L. (2008). Executive Coaching: an intervention, role function, or profession? *Consulting Psychology Journal: Practice & Research, 60*(1), 33-37.

Steiner, C. M. (1969). *A Warm Fuzzy Tale.* Retrieved 27th April 2009, from http://www.emotional-literacy.com/

Stern, L. R. (2004). Executive Coaching: A Working Definition. *Consulting Psychology Journal, 56,* 154-162.

Stoltzfus, T. (2008). *Coaching Questions: A Coaching Guide to Powerful Asking Skills.* Virginia Beach, VA: Coach 22.

surveymethods.com (2008). *Survey Software: Ask, Analyze, Improve* Retrieved 20th August 2008, from http://www.surveymethods.com/

Tang, K. Y. L. & Meuse, K. P. D. (2007). Literature Review of Media References on Coaching. *http://www.thefoundationofcoaching.org/*

Tashakkori, A. & Teddlie, C. (1998). *Mixed methodology : combining qualitative and quantitative approaches.* Thousand Oaks, Calif. ; London: Sage.

Thompson, T., Purdy, J. & Summers, D. B. (2008). A Five Factor Framework for Coaching Middle Managers. *Organizational Development Journal, 26*(3), 63.

Thomson, P. (2003). Introduction. In E. C. et. al (Ed.), *10 Things that keep CEOs Awake* (pp. xvii-xxii). London: McGraw Hill.

Tosey, P. & Mathison, J. (2003). Neuro-linguistic programming and learning theory: a response. *Curriculum Journal, 14*(3), 371-388.

Viadero, D. (2005). 'Mixed Methods' Research Examined. *Education Week, 24*(20), 1-20.

Whitmore, J. S. (2002). *Coaching for performance : growing people, performance and purpose* (3rd ed.). London: Nicholas Brealey.

Wittgenstein, L. (1958). *Philosophical Investigations.* Oxford: Blackwell.

Chapter 11

Bonus Chapter: Coaching Excellence

This paper was written in 2007 at the beginning of my 'masters journey'. It was during the production of this paper that my interest in the linguistic dimension of executive coaching developed.

What makes a great Executive Coach?

Against what set of competencies and capabilities will I identify the strengths in my own coaching practice and identify development opportunities?

The coaching industry is relatively new and there is much information available about coaching techniques and tools. Both coaching schools and accrediting bodies are eager to publish a set of competencies that a new coach should gain. However there is relatively little advanced training or even models of excellence in coaching.

The main outcome from this Action Learning Question is to describe clearly and concisely a model of excellence of what makes a great executive coach. The purpose is to develop a framework for evaluating and developing my own coaching practice, but ultimately one that could be used by any coach.

My approach was initially to review and consolidate the competencies and standards from the major 4 US, European and UK independent accrediting coaching bodies into a framework of excellence.

Then I tested the validity of that framework by interviewing experienced executive coaches and reviewing what they have written about excellence of executive coaching. I was particularly interested in any differences between approaches in the US and UK, as the coaching industry is more mature in the US.

A mind map of the methodology used

I will know I have achieved this outcome when I feel that I have a suitable framework against which I can measure my own competencies and received positive feedback from my supervisor. I will exceed my outcome when experienced coaches also give me feedback that they believe this document would have great value for themselves and other coaches.

Introduction

The UK Coaching industry is still in its infancy and growing fast. Executive Coaching is an acceptable part of personnal and professional development for senior people. The market is becoming more aware of the value executive coaching can deliver, but there are moves to create standards and accreditation (Tulip 2006). There is a parallel with the issues facing psychologists in the 1960s and an urgent need for regulation (personeltoday.com 2005a 2006b). There is also recognition that it maybe a difficult task to define standards for executive coaching. (Hardingham 2005)

There are a number of coaching bodies that publish competency standards, the most prevalent bodies in the UK and US markets are:

- Association for Coaching (AC) (associationforcoaching.com 2007)

- European and Mentoring Coaching Council (EMCC) (emccouncil.org 2007)

- International Association of Coaches (IAC) (certifiedcoach.org 2007)

- International Coaching Federation (ICF) (coachfederation.org 2007)

There are significant differences between the way the bodies go about accrediting coaches and training schools:

Accreditation of	Coach	Training school	Words
AC	Yes	No	600
EMCC	No	Yes	200
IAC	Yes	No*	3,000
ICF	Yes	Yes	1750

* The IAC has its own on-line training course that prepares coaches for their accreditation.

There are significant differences in the philosophy underpinning the accreditation of these bodies. For example the EMCC standards seem to be focused on meeting the needs of academics to define how coaching is to be taught at different levels of accreditation, while the AC standards seem to be as open as possible to allow a broad spectrum of membership.

It was interesting to note that the US originated bodies seems to have much more detail about the process of coaching than the UK bodies. For example – the ICF specifies a coach "Is able to move back and forth between the big picture of where the client is heading, setting a context for what is being discussed and where the client wishes to go" while the AC says "The coach demonstrates good listening and clarifying skills."

There were significant differences in the volume of information provided to support the accrediting process from the 200 words from the EMCC to the 3,000 words that the IAC uses to describe its new Coaching Masteries. It was interesting to note that both replaced much longer documents (2,200 and 23,000 words respectively).

The first step was to create a meta-model of the competency standards. Initial analysis of the categories used by each body revealed that the AC categories seemed to be at the highest level. Then grouping all the others categories within them resulted in the following map:

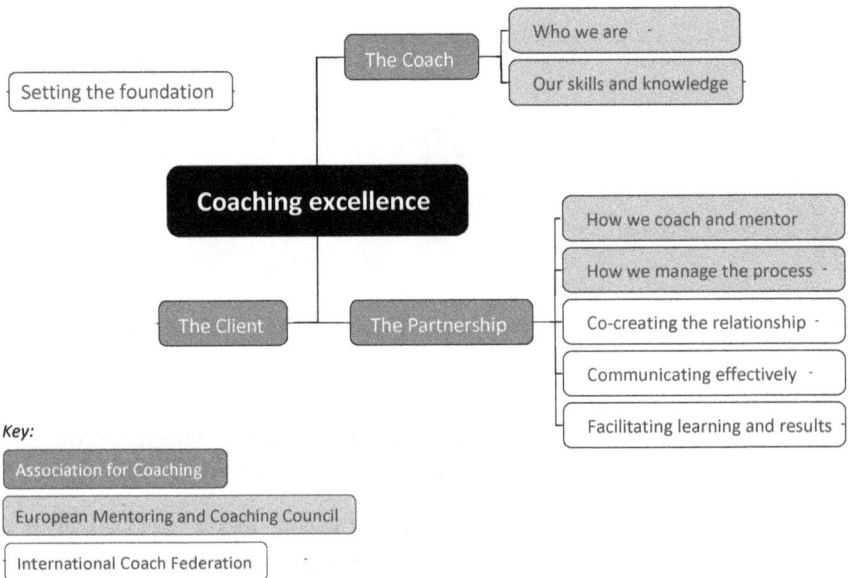

The Coach

Who we are

Setting the foundation

Our skills and knowledge

Coaching excellence

How we coach and mentor

How we manage the process

The Client — The Partnership

Co-creating the relationship

Communicating effectively

Facilitating learning and results

Key:

Association for Coaching

European Mentoring and Coaching Council

International Coach Federation

During the next stage of the analysis I concluded that two changes were necessary to the categories. The first was that there was an important dimension that the ICF called "setting the foundation", that together with other competencies from other bodies could be represented under a separate category called "Professional Practice".

The second change was that the category the AC call "The Partnership" includes both the relationship between the coach and the client; and what occurs during a coaching session. I considered splitting this category into two but concluded that simply calling it "Coaching" made the model clearer.

A detailed analysis of the competency maps created a new model of excellence, The 13 Dimensions of Coaching Excellence (shown below).

The final step was to compare the meta model with the research and conduct interviews with experienced executive coaches. A discussion of the results of that research follows.

Professional Practice	The Coach	The Client	Coaching	
How will a great executive coach structure their practice?	What is the identity of a great executive coach?	How does a great executive coach view the client?	What does a great executive coach do in a coaching program?	
Professionalism	Identity	Positive regard	Trust	Feedback
Contracting	Development	Independence	Presence	Approaches, Models & Process
			Active Listening	Systemic
			Questioning	

The 13 Dimensions of Coaching Excellence
© 2007 William Pennington

The 13 Dimensions of Coaching Excellence

The Professional Practice

Professionalism

All the accrediting bodies agree that it is important to meet ethical guidelines and professional standards. The AC goes further, suggesting awareness of your own philosophy, approach and ethics.

The AC and ICF agree that a clear understanding of what differentiates coaching from other modalities is required. However one executive coach in the US defines coaching as a "euphemism for psychotherapeutic intervention" and suggests the minimum time a coach should work with a client is 2-5 years. (Siegel 2005). All the professional accrediting bodies argue that an executive coach needs to know the boundaries of their practice and therefore when and how to refer clients on for psychotherapy, counselling or other intervention.

Many of the issues that I have observed executive coaches take to group supervision are around the area of integrity and ethics, they are looking to unravel the boundaries and complex issues around the sponsor (Human Resources), the stakeholder (line manager) and the client (coachee) in an organisation. These ethical dilemmas and how well they are resolved seem to define an excellent executive coach and it has been suggested that ethics should be placed above both training and professional accreditation. (de Jong 2006)

I have concluded that a great executive coach must have a professional philosophy and approach together with a clear vision of their ethics and possess the integrity, honesty and sincerity to put these into practice.

Contracting

It is important to start by defining what exactly is contracting. The AC talks about the comprehensive contractual agreement that is made with all stakeholders. In more depth it can be defined as the goals, roles and accountability of each party. (Sherman and Freas 2004)

The group of experienced executive coaches (DBM Focus Group 2006) use contracting as a process that enables them to deliver value to the organisation and the individual and be recognised for this. During this process they establish the agreed outcomes, the evaluation, stakeholder management, the guidelines for how the relationship will be managed and the logistics. This is an opportunity for the coach to determine if they believe they can facilitate the client (coachee) to achieve their objectives and those of the organisation.

The EMCC and ICF both include elements of managing the commercial relationship in this area, such as fees and commercial contract. It could be concluded that these are dimensions of being an effective business person rather than an effective coach.

An excellent coach will know how to structure an effective coaching partnership and a number of models have been put forward to enable a coach to create a viable contract that creates the ground rules of a coaching program. (Morgan, Marshall & Goldsmtih 2005; Tulpa 2006)

The Coach

Identity

Identity is asking the question "Who am I?" and has been described as:

> We answer this question by how we respond to life from moment to moment. When we are centered, present in our bodies and connected with ourselves and the world around us, we become naturally in touch with our life's purpose and meaning. (Dilts & Bacon 2007)

The EMCC describes this as self -encompassing self-belief, self-awareness, self-management and integrity, while the AC also talks about self-awareness but goes into more depth suggesting awareness and management of one's own values, emotional intelligence and map of the world are important.

'High Performance Coaching' is an NLP model of the most successful executive coaches (Breen & Percival 2004). They define not only the skills and behaviours of the leading executive coaches, but also the attitude. They described the inner brilliance that you identify not only in clients but in yourself as the coach.

One experienced executive coach talks about a balance with the client and that a great coach must be "self aware enough that he or she can maintain a distinct identity while fully engaged at an intellectual level. The coach succeeds by seeing the client succeed while never putting his or her personality ahead of the players." (Prahalad 2005).

Another says that executive coaches must "know themselves" and that "self awareness allows a coach to step aside from his or her own needs and be fully focused on the client." (Garfinkle 2005)

I have concluded that a great executive coach will be clear about and true to their values, identity and purpose, but will be able to put these aside as necessary to ensure the best possible coaching takes place for the client.

Development

The US accrediting bodies have little to say about development in their competencies. The IAC leave this to a paragraph in their ethics. The ICF imply a program of development with their various levels of accreditation and mastery of their range of competencies. Contrasting that with the EMCC that specifies a long list of skills and knowledge that a coach should have communication skills of listening, questioning, feedback, style and language; technical skills such as planning, systems thinking, artistic and creative skills; knowledge of learning theory, therapeutic approaches, psychological and psychotherapy models; and experience of corporate life, OD theory and management/leadership. They describe in more detail for training organisations by specifying how much knowledge a coach should have at each level, for example specifying the number of psychological models and OD theory that a "Master" coach should have learnt.

When I contrast that with the evidence from the 100+ experienced executive coaches interviewed or studied for this paper, I noticed there is a huge diversity in the quantity and mix of knowledge they possess. I also notice that clients and coaching employers make their own judgments about the experience and knowledge that is most relevant for them. For some a senior executive career is a pre-requisite for delivering executive coaching, for others a psychological degree and psychotherapy background is vital.

In contrast the AC specifies that a coach should undertake personal and professional development and simply described the steps of that process and mention supervision as a critical part. A recent report by the CIPD concluded that it was "the pivotal link between theory and coaching practice". They also concluded there are enormous benefits for organisations in getting better value from executive coaching. (Hawkins & Schwenk 2006) Coaching suppliers are also recognising this need and specifying that their coaches should have supervision. (DBM Focus Group 2006; Giber 2005)

Morgan, Harkins and Goldsmith (2006) put forward a very different 27 point model of the technical skills, experience and background, and coaching attributes that a "best practice coach" should have. They do not mention models, theories or systems but the pragmatic observations of the top 50 executive coaches in the US. One of the most relevant here is "A best practice coach has a keen knowledge where his or her experience starts and stops and how that will match the clients needs".

I have concluded that a great executive coach will be on a continuous journey of development and learning, gaining insight through self-reflection, supervision and other forms of evaluation. This will be in the context of what clients, suppliers and the markets need.

The Client

Positive Regard

This dimension encompasses competencies from all the accrediting bodies; they talk about belief in others, valuing diversity, acceptance and validation, respect for client, etc. A recurring theme is having Empathy and Belief.

> Empathy is the action of understanding, being aware of, being sensitive to, and vicariously experiencing the feelings, thoughts, and experience of another of either the past or present without having the feelings, thoughts, and experience fully communicated in an objectively explicit manner. (Merriam-Webster 2007)

The evidence from experienced coaches suggests going further and talk about caring more for the person than the program and honouring the humanity of the coachee (Ulrich 2005) (Sherman 2005)

Belief, but the question is belief of what? The EMCC simply suggests "others", while the AC suggests "potential and capability", the IAC also talk about the client's potential and holding them in high esteem while the ICF talk about respect for the client's personal being.

That is a theme that one experienced coach expanded on even further by asking the question about the 'anthropology' of a coach.

> "This is a deeper question than one of philosophy or technique. Is it asking "What do you believe about human beings? Where did we come from? Where do we find ourselves? and Where are we going?" (Leider 2005)

I have concluded that a great executive coach will have unconditional positive regard for their client. They will recognise their potential, believe in and empower them while maintaining complete empathy with the whole person and see their world as if it was their own.

Independence

The EMCC explicitly suggests "supporting independence" while the AC and IAC go into more depth by describing how a coach should encourage self-belief, inspire curiosity support self determined learning, facilitate setting and keeping clear intentions as well as provide feedback and celebration of progress.

A coach may create "not-to-do lists" and action plans for their clients and hold them accountable for results but it is important not to create co-dependent relationships. (Little 2005)

There is conflicting views on whether a coach is a teacher or not. If the role of the teacher is to have the answers and the role of a coach to have the questions, where should a great coach sit? (Whitmore 2003; Downey 2002; Burke 2005)

The client remains independent from the coach, always keeping ownership of the content but acknowledges there are times when the coach will have something to contribute "with permission". (Bresser & Wilson 2006)

My own experience is that as I become a more experienced coach, I have found it useful to share knowledge that I possess with my clients. But I have also experienced times when this teaching even with permission has in hindsight, not been beneficial to the coaching relationship.

I have concluded that a great executive coach will foster independence, empowering the client to take full responsibility for their own results. They will recognise when they have useful knowledge that can add to the client's situation without compromising the coaching relationship.

Coaching

Trust

All the accrediting bodies talk about establishing and maintaining trust at the core of the coaching relationship. They use a range of words and concepts associated with this including mutual respect, rapport, confidentiality, safe and supportive, intimacy, firm connection, non-judgmental, acceptance, values diversity, et al.

When asked in a survey of more than 100 clients the qualities they look for in a coach, the top rated answer was a coach is "trustworthy and honest". (Morgan, Harkins & Goldsmith 2005)

A critical aspect of successful coaching is that the coach will build trust quickly. (Morgan 2005) In a focus group of top UK executive coaches the view was that the key to gaining trust is through credibility, rapport and commitment to the client. (DBM Focus Group 2006)

The IAC suggests that the client feels safe to tell their deepest fears without judgment. My experience suggests the client will feel able to expose their dreams, their fears, their hopes, their weaknesses and their strengths without judgment. Or with judgment they can trust.

I have concluded that a great executive coach will be able to quickly build and develop trust with clients. They will be fully aware of the impact of their approaches on the coaching relationship.

Presence

The concept of "presence" is one that appears only in the ICF and IAC competencies, further analysis of these descriptions reveal there are internal and external dimensions:

The internal dimension is described by the ICF as "dancing in the moment". The IAC description is very close to that of Active Listening (see below), but with evidence from experienced coaches that maintaining focus and concentration can be a major challenge with some clients leads me to conclude that it would be difficult, if not impossible to get and maintain trust or to practice active listening if a coach was not fully present in the session. (DBM Focus Group 2006)

Internal presence is more than just the attention you bring to a client, but also that you leave behind your own agenda and ego. (Prahalad 2005; Morgan 2005)

The description of the external dimension to presence given by the ICF and IAC use words such as open, flexible, confident, intuitive, lightness, energy, holistic, space, et al. to describe the "place" that a coach must create for the client in order for the most effective coaching to occur.

One experienced executive coach described this as a critical dimension where a coach needs to be able to "carry the room" so the client believes the coaching will help. (Tracy 2005)

I have concluded that a great executive coach will manage their own state to be fully present with the client at all times, leaving their own ego and agenda out of the coaching and create the most effective place for amazing coaching to occur.

Active Listening

This is the one competency that all training courses, every certification standard and every book on coaching cites as being the main core skill required for coaching. Certainly all four accrediting bodies selected for this study and all the coaches who expressed an opinion agreed.

Taking all these definitions together, active listening is the fusion of hearing every word that a client says – precisely as he says it, giving that meaning from both directly what has been said and what has not been said, and placing it all in context while aligning it with other non-verbal signals.

It would not come as any surprise therefore that some coaches believe this is the single most important skill for a coach. (Bartlett 2005; Bolt 2005)

I have concluded that a great executive coach will gain the maximum possible insight into their clients by hearing, seeing, feeling and knowing more.

Questioning

The accrediting bodies all agree that asking powerful questions is an important competency. The AC suggests this is for the purpose of identifying areas for development, while the IAC suggests this is for the alignment of purpose, vision and mission, to identify key values and needs and identify blocks. The ICF stress the importance of the connection between powerful questioning and active listening and for the purpose of evoking discovery and creating insight, commitment or action.

It is remarkably difficult to find any coach who talks much about questions. Even the 'The Queen of Powerful Questions' says "You want a coach who has the ability to not just listen well, but to listen for." (Baker 2005)

One experienced coach suggested that the skill of appreciative enquiry is useful i.e. the ability to go deep into an issue while keeping a watch for the solution. The skill of asking questions is more of an art than science that improves with experience. (Helgesen 2005)

I have concluded that great executive coaches will, not only be able to ask the right question at the right time but understand when to use feedback or challenge.

Feedback

All the accrediting bodies agree that feedback is an important process to provide information, summarise, reflect, re-iterate, paraphrase or provide clarity and understanding. The IAC suggests that this should be done in clear, articulated, appropriate and respectful ways.

Both ICF and IAC talk about feedback that challenges and the focus group talked about how to create the right level of distress for the comfortable. (DBM Focus Group 2006)

One coach quoting John Gardner said:

> "Pity the leader caught between unloving critics and uncritical lovers …what leaders need are 'loving critics'" (Kouzes 2005)

There is little said about the situation where a coach does none of this and says nothing at all! Only the IAC talks about 'productive silence' allowing silence to give the client space for discovery. And what about non-verbal communication? Most of the accreditation bodies talk about being aware of a client's non-verbal communication, but only the IAC talks about using non-verbal communication in return.

I have concluded that a great executive coach will be able to find the right balance between challenge and respect, provide the appropriate feedback, use productive silence and have the appropriate style in the moment.

Bringing together Active Listening, Questioning and Feedback

The IAC encompass the whole process of active listening, questioning and feedback as "Inviting Possibilities" - a process of exploring and discovering by curiosity, courage, openness and trust.

One experienced coach helps leaders discover their purpose and build on strengths while managing weaknesses" Another says "In the most mature coaching relationship ...the coaching flows from a continuous creative conversation." (Leider 2005); Anderson 2005)

I have concluded that a great executive coach will have mastered three essential skills of Active Listening, Questioning and Feedback and have integrated them together seamlessly.

Approaches, Models and Process

The coaching industry brings together an eclectic mix of many disciplines in one place; there is NLP, personal development, psychological and therapeutic modalities, sports coaching, counselling, et al. In talking to and reading about experienced and successful coaches I have observed that each has collected a mix of favourite tools, techniques and models they use in their practice.

The EMCC and ICF talk about the understanding and management of a client's goals, attitudes, beliefs, values, behaviours, motivation and actions.   The High Performance Coaching model takes most of these elements and maps them to a visual guide that guides the student through the coaching process. However my experience has been that it rapidly becomes something you refer to as a diagnostic and other experienced coaches have commented that models become internalised, so that they become an unconscious process. (Alexander 2006; Breen & Percival 2005)

I have concluded that a great executive coach will have developed approaches, models and processes to be a seamless part of their practice.

Systemic approach

There is relatively little said by the accrediting bodies about a systemic approach which acknowledges executive coaching takes place in the context of a complex system, i.e. the organisation. The EMCC suggests that a business focus and political awareness are important competencies coupled with corporate knowledge and organisational development theory.

It is perhaps an obvious pre-supposition of executive coaching that the primary objective should be to deliver the maximum value to the organisation.   Or perhaps it is not so obvious! One coaching supplier interviews over 100 coaches a year and only finds a handful who continually asks themselves "Why am I in this room?", i.e. what is the benefit to the organisation? (DBM Focus Group 2006)

An experienced and very successful coach says he now spends most of his time with the key stakeholders around his clients and as a result gets dramatically better outcomes. (Goldsmith 2005).

I have concluded that a great executive coach will be aware of the systemic influence on their clients and the coaching program. They will look for ways they can engage with stakeholders in the organisation to make them an integral part of the intervention.

Conclusions

In my research and interviews I found much that has been written about the science of executive coaching, but less about the art. For example how would intuition fit into this model and what other factors are missing that could make up the art?

I have concluded that a great executive coach recognises that it is a journey towards mastery! But it is not about **recognising** the journey but about **taking** the journey.

> *"A coach, like a leader, can be developed if she/he possesses the original passion. But this is a personal journey more than an educational attainment. Coaching accreditation programs probably can't teach the art of coaching any more that golf instruction can teach the art of golf. Skills can be learned and techniques replicated, but true understanding only comes from carefully honed practice in real-world situations."*

(Morgan, Harkins and Goldsmith 2005)

I will use these 13 competencies as useful markers on the chartered paths that lie ahead in my development as an executive coach. But I also believe there will be uncharted waters too; in our understanding of human capability, creativity and purpose and in the practice of how we, as great executive coaches, make them work for our clients better.

References

AC Integrated Coaching Competency Framework (2007). Retrieved 2nd May 2007 from http://www.associationforcoaching.com/

Anderson, S. (2005). Career / Life Coaching. In H. Morgan, P. Harkins and M. Goldsmith (Eds.) *The Art and Practice of Leadership Coaching.* (pp. 110-112). New Jersey: Wiley.

Alexander, G. (2006) Behavioural Coaching: The GROW Model In J. Passmore (Ed.) *Excellence in Coaching - Industry Guide,* (pp.61-72). London: Kogan Page.

Baker, M. (2005). Career / Life Coaching. In H. Morgan, P. Harkins and M. Goldsmith (Eds.) *The Art and Practice of Leadership Coaching.* (pp. 117-120). New Jersey: Wiley.

Barnes, K. (2005). Career / Life Coaching. In H. Morgan, P. Harkins and M. Goldsmith (Eds.) *The Art and Practice of Leadership Coaching.* (pp. 85-87). New Jersey: Wiley.

Bartlett C.A. (2005). Coaching the Top Team. In H. Morgan, P. Harkins and M. Goldsmith (Eds.) *The Art and Practice of Leadership Coaching.* (pp. 199-202). New Jersey: Wiley.

Bolt, J. (2005). Coaching for Leadership Development. In H. Morgan, P. Harkins and M. Goldsmith (Eds.) *The Art and Practice of Leadership Coaching.* (pp. 143-146). New Jersey: Wiley.

Breen, M. & Percival, E. (2004). *High Performance Coaching Course Manual.*

Bresser, F. & Wilson, C. (2006) What is Coaching? In J. Passmore (Ed.) *Excellence in Coaching - Industry Guide,* (pp.9-25). London: Kogan Page.

Burke, W.W. (2005). Thinking Strategically During Change. In H. Morgan, P. Harkins and M. Goldsmith (Eds.) *The Art and Practice of Leadership Coaching.* (pp. 159-161). New Jersey: Wiley.

Coaches sow seeds of chaos as business stays in the dark (2006, January) Rerieved 2nd May 2007 from http://www.personneltoday.com/

Coaching profession needs to be regulated (2006, January). Retrieved 2nd May 2007 from http://www.personneltoday.com/

DBM Focus Group. (2006). 7 UK Executive coaches and 5 client representatives.

De Jong, A. (2006) Coaching Ethics: integrity in the moment of choice. In J. Passmore (Ed.) *Excellence in Coaching - Industry Guide*, (pp.191-202). London: Kogan Page.

Dilts, R. & Bacon, D. (2007). *Coaching at the Identity Level*. Retrieved 2nd May 2007 from http://www.nlpu.com/

Downley, M. (2003) *Effective Coaching*. 2nd Edition. Mason: Thomson Texere.

EMCC Competency Framework (2007), Retrieved 2nd May 2nd from http://www.emccouncil.org/

Garfinkle, C.K. (2005). Career/Life Coaching. In H. Morgan, P. Harkins and M. Goldsmith (Eds.) *The Art and Practice of Leadership Coaching*. (pp. 112-115). New Jersey: Wiley.

Giber, D. (2005). Coaching for Leadership Development. In H. Morgan, P. Harkins and M. Goldsmith (Eds.) *The Art and Practice of Leadership Coaching*. (pp. 146-149). New Jersey: Wiley.

Goldsmith, M. (2005). Changing Leadership Behavior. In H. Morgan, P. Harkins and M. Goldsmith (Eds.) *The Art and Practice of Leadership Coaching*. (pp. 56-61). New Jersey: Wiley.

Hardingham, A. (2005, September), *CIPD People management magazine*, p. 45

Hawkins P. & Schwenk G. (2006) *Coaching Supervision, Maximising The Potential Of Coaching*. Retreived 2nd May 2007 from http://www.cipd.co.uk/

Helgesen, S. (2005). Coaching Anthropology. In H. Morgan, P. Harkins and M. Goldsmith (Eds.) *The Art and Practice of Leadership Coaching*. (pp. 161-165). New Jersey: Wiley.

IAC Coaching Masteries (2007). Retrieved 2nd May 2007 from http://www.certifiedcoach.org/

ICF Professional Coaching Core Competencies. (2007). Retrieved 2nd May 2007 from http://www.coachfederation.org/

Kouzes, J. (2005). Coaching for Credibility. In H. Morgan, P. Harkins and M. Goldsmith (Eds.) *The Art and Practice of Leadership Coaching*. (pp. 61-66). New Jersey: Wiley.

Leider R.J. (2005). The Inherent Dilemmas of Career/Life Coaching. In H. Morgan, P. Harkins and M. Goldsmith (Eds.) *The Art and Practice of Leadership Coaching*. (pp. 88-93). New Jersey: Wiley.

Little, B. (2005). Coaching Leaders / Behavioural Coaching. In H. Morgan, P. Harkins and M. Goldsmith (Eds.) *The Art and Practice of Leadership Coaching*. (pp. 83-85). New Jersey: Wiley.

Merriam-Webster (2007) Retrieved 2nd May 2007 from http://www.m-w.com/

Morgan, H. (2005). Coaching Leaders / Behavioural Coaching. In H. Morgan, P. Harkins and M. Goldsmith (Eds.) *The Art and Practice of Leadership Coaching*. (pp. 78-80). New Jersey: Wiley.

Morgan, H., Harkins, P. & Goldsmith, M. (2005) *The Art and Practice of Leadership Coaching*. New Jersey: Wiley.

Prahalad, C.K. (2005). The Competative Demands on Today's Leaders. In H. Morgan, P. Harkins and M. Goldsmith (Eds.) *The Art and Practice of Leadership Coaching*. (pp. 190-195). New Jersey: Wiley.

Sherman, S. and Freas, A. (2004, November) The wild west of executive coaching, *Harvard Business Review*.

Sherman, S. (2005). Coaching for Organisational Change. In H. Morgan, P. Harkins and M. Goldsmith (Eds.) *The Art and Practice of Leadership Coaching*. (pp. 176-179). New Jersey: Wiley.

Siegel, K. (2005). Coaching Leaders/Behavioral Coaching. In H. Morgan, P. Harkins and M. Goldsmith (Eds.) *The Art and Practice of Leadership Coaching*. (pp. 80-83). New Jersey: Wiley.

Tracey, B. (2005). Career / Life Coaching. In H. Morgan, P. Harkins and M. Goldsmith (Eds.) *The Art and Practice of Leadership Coaching*. (pp. 106-110). New Jersey: Wiley.

Tulip, S. (2006, September 14th) Lighting the way: Coaching market review, *CIPD People Management magazine* p. 44.

Tulpa, K. (2006). Coaching within Organisations. In J. Passmore (Ed.) *Excellence in Coaching - Industry Guide*, (pp.26-43). London: Kogan Page.

Ulrich, D. (2005). Vision, Style and Strategy. In H. Morgan, P. Harkins and M. Goldsmith (Eds.) *The Art and Practice of Leadership Coaching*. (pp. 74-76). New Jersey: Wiley.

Whitmore, J. (2002). *Coaching for Performance*. 3rd Edition. London: Nicholas Brealey Publishing.

Global Survey

The global on-line survey was launched 17th November 2008 and within minutes the emails started coming in! In the first 24 hours, coaches with over 2,000 years of experience had responded. Day by day the number of respondents increased and by the end of the first week, over 1,000 coaches had taken part. Over the next few weeks, I answered hundreds and hundreds of emails. It all felt amazing!

Many sent kind greetings and I was warmed by the community of coaches around the globe, a typical email was :

Good morning, William

I just completed your online survey. Please accept my congratulations on a job well done. You survey was clear and concise – as was the accompanying white paper. This is quite a feat since you are apparently doing a global survey.

Please accept my best wishes in your future endeavours.

When the survey closed on the 15th December over 1,800 coaches had completed the survey. I cannot thank those who took part enough, as without their investment of time, thought and energy, there would have been no dissertation, no masters degree and no book!

One coach who was invited to take part asked me: "Why should I contribute my learning and experience to your development?" My response was that in my experience, when you share your learning and experience you actually get more back. I hope that all those who took part in this, the largest executive coaching survey will get much more back.

Executive Coaching & Language

Page 1 - Welcome and a little background about you

Welcome to this short confidential survey that will take around 10-15 minutes to complete.

This survey is part of my MA research project at Kingston University in the United Kingdom. The research is conducted under the Ethical Guidelines published by the University. If you would like to receive a copy, please contact me at wp@chicoaching.com.

The purpose is to ask the questions: "What is executive coaching?" and "What are the language behaviours used?".

Please note that my research is about coaching in the English language. This has informed some of the questions below and also why this survey is only being conducted in English!

Thank you for taking the time to complete this survey.

William Pennington
Chi Coaching

1. Where are you living now?

   ○ Australia ○ Canada ○ Ireland ○ New Zealand ○ South Africa ○ UK ○ US
   ○ If other, please specify

2. Where else have you lived? (tick any that apply)

   ☐ Australia ☐ Canada ☐ Ireland ☐ New Zealand ☐ South Africa ☐ UK ☐ US
   ☐ If other, please specify

3. What is your mother tongue?

   ○ English ○ French ○ German ○ Mandarin Chinese ○ Russian ○ Spanish
   ○ If other, please specify

4. In which language do you primarily coach?

   ○ English ○ French ○ German ○ Mandarin Chinese ○ Russian ○ Spanish
   ○ If other, please specify

5. What is your business status as a coach?

   ○ Own my own business (sole trader)

   ○ Own a business with others (Ltd, Inc, LLP, etc.)

   ○ Employed by an organization to coach their people (internal)

   ○ Employed by an organization to deliver coaching to their customers

   ○ If other, please specify

6. What was your background before becoming a coach?

- ○ Business - executive
- ○ Business - consulting
- ○ Occupational psychology
- ○ Clinical psychology
- ○ If other, please specify

7. In which of these are you actively engaged in your practice? (tick any that apply)

- ☐ Executive Coaching
- ☐ Life Coaching
- ☐ Business Coaching
- ☐ Consulting
- ☐ Teaching
- ☐ Psychotherapy
- ☐ Counselling
- ☐ Facilitation
- ☐ Mediation
- ☐ If other, please specify

Page 2 - Defining Executive Coaching

8. Who do you understand receives "Executive Coaching"? (select any that apply)

- [ ] Board Members, Directors, CXOs
- [ ] Senior Managers
- [ ] Managers at all levels
- [ ] Specialists without management responsibility
- [ ] Anyone in an organization
- [ ] Anyone
- [ ] If any other, please specify

This section will ask you some questions to gauge your understanding of the definition of Executive Coaching.

9. On a scale of 1 to 10; How much do you rate each of the following definitions? (where 10 means you completely agree)

EXECUTIVE COACHING IS . . .

	1	2	3	4	5	6	7	8	9	10
a helping relationship	○	○	○	○	○	○	○	○	○	○
a form of consulting	○	○	○	○	○	○	○	○	○	○
a branch of organizational psychology	○	○	○	○	○	○	○	○	○	○
a facilitated learning process	○	○	○	○	○	○	○	○	○	○
one-to-one counselling	○	○	○	○	○	○	○	○	○	○
underpinned by psychotherapeutic theories	○	○	○	○	○	○	○	○	○	○
on a continuum between counselling and consulting	○	○	○	○	○	○	○	○	○	○

10. How much do you agree with these statements about Executive Coaching and Executive Coaches?

	Strongly Agree	Agree	Neutral	Disagree	Strongly Disagree
"Executive Coaching takes place within a triadic relationship between a coach, executive and organization"	○	○	○	○	○
"An Executive Coach acts as a facilitative change-agent working primarily one-to-one with an Executive"	○	○	○	○	○
"An Executive Coach works in a collaborative equal partnership with an Executive"	○	○	○	○	○
"The purpose of Executive coaching is to create sustained change in the Executive's skills, behaviour and performance so that both the Executive and their organization get ultimate benefit"	○	○	○	○	○

11. Any comments on these statements?

Page 3 - Language skills in Executive Coaching

This section will ask you to think about language behaviours in the practice of Executive Coaching, for example, listening.

If you undertake different types of coaching please focus on what happens only in the context of Executive Coaching.

12. How much time does a coach spend speaking and listening during an Executive Coaching session?

Please fill in all three boxes (including a 0 if that's your answer)
The sum of all values entered must equal 100.

Listening

Speaking

Other

13. If other, what is taking place then?

14. **On a scale of 1 to 10**, Rate how relevant each language behaviour is in Executive Coaching. (where 10 is totally relevant)

	1	2	3	4	5	6	7	8	9	10
telling	○	○	○	○	○	○	○	○	○	○
instructing	○	○	○	○	○	○	○	○	○	○
giving advice	○	○	○	○	○	○	○	○	○	○
explaining	○	○	○	○	○	○	○	○	○	○
being a role model	○	○	○	○	○	○	○	○	○	○
offering guidance	○	○	○	○	○	○	○	○	○	○
giving feedback	○	○	○	○	○	○	○	○	○	○
providing ideas	○	○	○	○	○	○	○	○	○	○
questioning	○	○	○	○	○	○	○	○	○	○
paraphrasing	○	○	○	○	○	○	○	○	○	○
summarizing	○	○	○	○	○	○	○	○	○	○
reflecting	○	○	○	○	○	○	○	○	○	○
listening	○	○	○	○	○	○	○	○	○	○

15. What other language behaviours do you think are important?

16. In your own practice of Executive Coaching, place each language behaviour in the order that you use them.

Please use 1 for the most, 2 for the second, 3 for the third etc until you get to 7 for the least? Use each number 1,2,3,4,5,6,7 only once.
Rank the following items using numbers from 1 to 7.

reflecting, summarizing and paraphrasing

questioning

feedback

providing ideas and guidance

being a role model

explaining and giving advice

telling and instructing

Page 4 - Language Models

This section is about language models that you know, have learned and use.

17. Please consider each language model and indicate your knowledge or use of each in your executive coaching practice.

	don't know of it	heard of it	learned it	use it a little	use it a lot
appreciative enquiry	○	○	○	○	○
META model	○	○	○	○	○
Milton model	○	○	○	○	○
Meta programs	○	○	○	○	○
LAB profile	○	○	○	○	○
hypnotic language	○	○	○	○	○
clean language	○	○	○	○	○
metaphors	○	○	○	○	○
socratic questioning	○	○	○	○	○
open/closed questions	○	○	○	○	○
speech acts	○	○	○	○	○
meta-questions	○	○	○	○	○
question-centered therapy	○	○	○	○	○
cognitive linguistics	○	○	○	○	○

18. Any other language or questioning models that you have learned or use?

19. How do you use these language models in your Executive Coaching practice?

Page 5 - Your Practice

20. How much of your work time do you spend on these functions?

    Please fill in all three boxes (including a 0 if that's your answer)
    The sum of all values entered must equal 100.

    Executive Coaching

    Other coaching

    Other activities

21. How many years have you been practicing Executive Coaching?

    ◌ student

    ◌ less than 2 years

    ◌ between 2 and 5 years

    ◌ between 5 and 10 years

    ◌ over 10 years

22. Please provide more detailed information about the total experience in your career as a professional Executive Coach.

    You may only enter numbers or leave blank. Please add any comments below if you wish.

    Face-to-face hours of Executive Coaching

    Telephone hours of Executive Coaching

    Number of executive coachees

    Number of organizations

23. Please provide any feedback or comments you may have about this survey?

    Please click the submit below to complete your survey.

Survey Reliability and Validity

Reliability Checks Using Alternative Forms

The on-line survey contains the following pairs and trio of questions that check for reliability.

1) Questions 7 and 20 for a practicing executive coach.

2) Questions 9 and 10 for agreement on "facilitated learning process".

3) Questions 12 and 14 for correlation between the amount of time an executive coach listens and their ranking for the relevance of listening; for example, it was judged it would be highly unlikely that they spend more than 60% of their time doing something they considered irrelevant.

4) Questions 14 and 16 for correlation between how much questioning, feedback, telling and instructing were used and how relevant they were; for example, it was judged that an executive coach would be highly unlikely to rank questioning as their least used and most relevant.

5) Questions 20, 21 and 22 for data regarding an executive coach's practice.

Coding and Data Cleaning

The cleaning process used the following process:

A. Qualitative data provided in *other* was reviewed and coded appropriately – in some cases answers were provided that matched existing codes, in others it was determined there were sufficient cases to create a new distinct code.

B. Inconsistent or incomplete data was either re-coded or removed. In particular the questions using a *10 point numerical rating scale* included cases that had entered *non-answers* i.e. all the same number and some cases indicated that their answers were not valid. Answers to 27 cases were removed.

C. Inconsistent responses to pairs of questions were identified and further analysis of comments determined if the answers to these cases should be removed. The answers to a total of 76 cases were removed.

D. Statistical analysis highlighted outliners, thus answers to a total of 22 cases were removed.

The impact on this process on each question in the survey is as follows:

Question 1: Where are you living now?:

A. Other -> Europe (6), Other (4)

Question 2: Where else have you lived?

A. Other -> Europe (125), Other (144)

Question 3: What is your mother tongue?

A. No changes.

Question 4: In which language do you primarily coach?

A.   No changes.

Question 5: How do you do business as a coach?

A.   90 cases answered *other* of which 82 cases provided qualitative data that could be coded into the pre-defined categories.

Question 6: What was your background before coming a coach?

A.   This question provided the most *other* responses (400), however 111 cases provided qualitative information to allow accurate coding into existing categories. In particular, cases had an executive background but in a non-profit making organisation, or held a management position but did not consider to be an *executive*.   Therefore the category *Business Executive* includes those cases who held a leadership position in any organisation.

In addition there were a significant number of cases that justified two new groups *Education* with 53 cases and *HR, Learning and Development, Training* with 66 cases.

Notes:

a.   Education specifically refers to those in academic environments.

b.   Training refers to those delivering training in a business context.

c.   HR Directors / Leaders were considered part of *Business – executive.*

Question 7: In which of these are you actively engaged in your practice?

A.   A significant number (198) of qualitative answers in *other* used terms *training, team coaching* or *leadership coaching* and these were coded as *teaching, facilitation* and *executive coaching* respectively.

Question 8: Who do you understand receives "executive coaching"? (select any that apply)

A.   94 cases answered *other* and provided qualitative information that could be coded by pre-existing categories.   15 Cases mentioned *business owners* and a new code was created.

191 cases selected only one option that could result in illogical results. For example, they selected *all managers* but not *senior managers*. The additional codes were added to these cases using the following mapping:

Answer 6 only = 1, 2, 3, 4, 5 and 6
Answer 5 only = 1, 2, 3, 4 and 5
Answer 3 only = 1, 2 and 3
Answer 2 only = 1 and 2

where:
6 = *Anyone*
5 = *Anyone in organisation*
4 = *Specialists in an organization*
3 = *Managers at all levels*
2 = *Senior Managers*
1 = *Board members, Directors, CxO*

Question 9: On a scale of 1-10, how much do you rate the following definitions? (where 10 means you completely agree)

B.   Answers from cases 877, 927, 953, 1302, 1470, 1596, 1694 and 1730 were removed.

D. Further analysis of outliners resulted in removal of the answers from cases 24, 103, 180, 484, 664, 685, 858, 1331, 1493, 1629 and 1697.

Question 10: How much do you agree with the following statements about executive coaching and executive coaches? (1=strongly agree, 5=strongly disagree)

C. Comparing the rating of the definition of an executive coach acts as a *facilitative change agent* and executive coaching as a *facilitated learning process* results in a small number of inconsistencies in the data. It was concluded that some cases reversed their answers to question 10 and these 13 cases 11, 17, 93, 116, 308, 419, 506, 649, 984, 1043, 1161, 1237, 1654, 1707 and 1824 were therefore removed.

D. Further analysis of outliners resulted in removal of the answers from case 484.

Question 11: Any comments on these statements?

Analysed qualitatively.

Quetsion 12: How much time does a coach spend speaking and listening during an executive coaching session?

A. Cases 63, 100, 193, 209, 245, 334, 391, 395, 419, 447, 458, 512, 609, 669, 936, 977, 1080, 1105, 1121, 1216, 1247, 1277, 1381, 1456, 1479, 1579 and 1634 provided qualitative data in Question 13 that required re-coding of the percentages, many for example separated questioning from speaking.

C. Comparing a case's answer for this question with that for question 14, it was concluded that cases 256, 549, 686, 761, 1093, 1316 and 1677, had probably reversed their answers and were removed.   It was noted that the question lists *speaking* and *listening* in a different order than the data input section.

D.   Outliner analysis resulted in cases 89, 402, 485, 527, 528, 682, 832, 1071, 1082, 1243, 1331, 1523, 1730, 1760 being removed.

Question 13: If other, what is taking place then?

Analysed qualitatively.

Question 14: On a scale of 1 to 10, rate how relevant each language behaviour is in the practice of executive coaching (where 10 is totally relevant).

B.   Answers from cases 199, 216, 321, 433, 686, 1036, 1134, 1183, 1407, 1479, 1505, 1545, 1625, 1727, 1784 and 1793 were removed.

Question 15: What other language behaviours do you think are important?

Analysed qualitatively.

Question 16: In your own practice of executive coaching, which of the following language behaviours do you use the most?

C.   This question proved to be a problem for many people, the system required input of ranking numbers from 1 to 7, but they could not manage to provide that input correctly. The researcher added clearer instructions to the question and changed the status to non compulsory.

However some cases still inputted the ranking in the reverse order, as their answers to this question was contradictory to the previous question. i.e. On question 14 they rated *telling* as 1 (irrelevant) and *questioning* as 10 (totally relevant) while in question 16 ranked *questioning* least used and *telling* most used. The answers from 54 cases 7, 25, 41, 60, 112, 114, 116, 188, 190,

229, 242, 297, 308, 361, 390, 413, 447, 459, 572, 603, 617, 689, 698, 827, 859, 897, 951, 953, 1130, 1169, 1196, 1295, 1297, 1271, 1319, 1368, 1398, 1435, 1458, 1466, 1511, 1586, 1611, 1624, 1628, 1648, 1688, 1695, 1697, 1700, 1707, 1778, 1790 and 1824 were removed.

Question 17: Please consider each language model and indicate your knowledge or use of each in your executive coaching practice.

B.   Answers from cases 1335, 673 and 1629 were removed.

Question 18: Any other language or questioning models that you have learnt or use?

Analysed qualitatively.

Question 19: How do you use these language models in your practice?

Analysed qualitatively.

Question 20: How much time do you spend working on these functions? % executive coaching vs % other coaching vs % other activities

No changes.

Question 21: How many years have you been practicing executive coaching?

No changes.

www.ingramcontent.com/pod-product-compliance
Lightning Source LLC
Chambersburg PA
CBHW020400100426
42812CB00001B/135